THE

BEASTS

OF

EPHESUS

THE

BEASTS

OF

EPHESUS

REV. JAMES BRAND, D.D.

Pastor, First Congregational Church,
Oberlin, Ohio

With an Introduction by

Rev. Francis E. Clark, D.D.,
President, United Society of Christian Endeavor

BRAND, JAMES

The Beasts of Ephesus (1892).—

Originally published in 1892
By The Advance Publishing Co., Chicago

Modern Edition © 2015 Full Well Ventures
ISBN-13: 978-1-62834-007-5
ISBN-10: 162834007X

"If after the manner of men I fought with the beasts of Ephesus, what doth it profit me? If the dead are not raised, let us eat and drink for tomorrow we die."

1 Corinthians 15:32.

TABLE OF CONTENTS

INTRODUCTION, *by Rev. Francis E. Clark.* 9

I INTRODUCTORY 11

II THE YOUNG CHRISTIAN AND THE CITY 19

III THE YOUNG CHRISTIAN AND MONEY 27

IV THE YOUNG CHRISTIAN AND BAD BOOKS 35

V THE YOUNG CHRISTIAN AND THE THEATER 45

VI THE YOUNG CHRISTIAN AND THE CARD TABLE 61

VII THE YOUNG CHRISTIAN AND CLUBS 69

VIII THE YOUNG CHRISTIAN AND THE POPULAR DANCE 77

IX THE YOUNG CHRISTIAN'S NIGHTS AND SUNDAYS 89

X THE YOUNG CHRISTIAN AND THE SABBATH 97

XI THE YOUNG CHRISTIAN AND SOCIAL PURITY 109

XII THE YOUNG CHRISTIAN AND MARKET INFIDELITY 119

XIII THE YOUNG CHRISTIAN AND THE MAJORITY 129

XIV THE YOUNG CHRISTIAN AND THE WEED 137

XV CONCLUSION — CHRIST'S APPEAL TO THE HEROISM OF YOUNG PEOPLE 161

INTRODUCTION

THIS IS a book that the times demand. The Beasts of Ephesus are still going about seeking whom they may devour. They change their form but not their natures. Every young person has to battle with these as did Paul. This book will enable them to discern the ravenous beasts even under the sheep's clothing and it will arm them for the fight with the panoply of God.

This is a book from the right source. It is evidently wrought out of a pastor's loving heart. It is written by one who has seen with pain, and sometimes with anguish, the beasts rending their victims, by one who has longed to leap into the arena and slay the monsters that are slaying the young. Only a pastor who has mourned over mangled lives and wasted possibilities in youth could have written such a book. There is in these chapters much of the "woe is me if" I write not this book. It is written not to satisfy a literary dilettantism, but a yearning love for young souls.

This is a temperate book. It does not denounce amusements in a wholesale, indiscriminate way. It does not mistake a mouse for a lion, or brandish its sword against a harmless hare. It chooses real and not imaginary evils and makes nice discriminations between a sin per se and the tendency and trend of an amusement which may lead to sin; basing its opposition upon rational and reasonable grounds that will commend themselves to the experiences and consciences of young people everywhere.

This is a strong book. In vigorous English the author grapples with many delicate subjects and never fails to make his meaning clear. The conventionalities of society life have not induced him to choose or pick phrases which are equivocal, or destitute of the fire of righteous indignation. The author sees underneath the surface the hideous, soul-blighting tendencies of some of these forms of social amusement, and strips off the mask which they wear in public.

From personal experience I know that some of the questions here treated; the card table, the theater, the popular dance, etc., perplex many young Christians more than any other problems of the day. Dr. Brand's plain and earnest words will do much to resolve their doubts, will furnish them with weapons of offense and defense against the sophist, and will brace their souls to resist the attacks of the enemy of all righteousness.

Above all, the author touches the right chord in appealing to the heroic element in Christian youths. Young people cannot be wheedled into the right, or coaxed into giving up the wrong, but he who writes to them "because ye are strong," he who recognizes the Christlike courage of every true young Christian; he who appeals to the highest manliness and womanliness in the young disciple and urges duty "for Christ's sake" will not write in vain. With such spiritual insight and strength has Dr. Brand written these stirring chapters. I wish that every young person in all the land might read them.

Francis E. Clark.
Boston, May 24, 1892.

CHAPTER I:
INTRODUCTORY

PAUL IS dead; but the Beasts of Ephesus are still alive. Their distinguishing characteristic is longevity. They belong to every age and clime. They will not cease to exist till the millennium comes. And every man and woman who proposes to be an out-and-out Christian, must enter the arena, as Paul did, and give them battle.

What were the Beasts of Ephesus? Beyond all reasonable doubt the Apostle's language in 1 Corinthians 15:32, was figurative, not literal. He meant that during his stay at Ephesus he had to contend with men and customs, ideas and influences, which were of such a nature that the battle was like that of a man fighting for life with wild beasts. This will seem to be the only reasonable interpretation when we remember on the one hand, that Paul's Roman citizenship would have saved him from the indignity of being sentenced to literal combat with beasts in the amphitheater; and on the other, if it had been a literal fight the case would surely have been mentioned by Luke in his account of Paul's work in that city. It is incredible that such an event could have been passed over in silence by a careful historian who did mention details far less important than that would have been.

Paul's thought was this: If, like the great mass of men, with no motive but that of the present earthly life, with no inspiration drawn from my relation to God and the hope of immortality, I have fought, as it were, with beasts here in Ephesus, what do I gain? What is the use? Why continue this struggle with the world, the flesh and the devil? If there is no immortal life beyond, then let us go with the world.

That this is his thought seems the more certain from the character of Ephesus itself. It was a city of "many adversaries," a great commercial center, lying at the junction of great roads which connected it with the interior and far east, as the sea did with the far west. It naturally brought together all the moral leprosy of the heathen world. Canon Farrar calls it "The Vanity Fair of Asia." Paul was daily confronted in his work with the bitter prejudice of money-grasping Jews, and ridiculed by the luxurious and licentious Greeks. The city was famous for its intellectual pride and its groveling superstition. It was honeycombed with sorcery and falsehood. The people lived for the attainment of creature comforts and the gratification of carnal passions. The vicinity of the great temple, with its hordes of male and female priests, "reeked with the congregated pollution of Asia." Everywhere were wrong views of morals and false maxims of life. The city was full of men who would sell even spiritual gifts any hour for money with which to gratify the flesh. No self-denial, no lofty spiritual aims, blank materialism, social corruption, prostituted art. "Ionia, the corruptness of Greece, Ephesus the corruptness of Ionia, the favorite scene of her most voluptuous love tales; the lighted theater of her most ostentatious sins." Along with all this, and embosoming it all, was the perpetual presence of great, dazzling, alluring, captivating material splendor and display.

In the midst of such scenes, that lonely man of God

had to live and work and fight. Here were the Beasts of Ephesus. And yet in the strength of his simple, sublime faith, sustained by the presence of Christ and the assurance of immortality, he was enabled to stand his ground and daily fling himself anew into the unending combat. When I am tempted, he seems to say, as I often am, to fall in with the common life of this godless city, and take my ease like other men, then I think of my mortal freedom; I think of the resurrection; I think of the throne of judgment; I think of eternal life; I think of communion with God; I remember the life, the love, the peace, the glory of Christ, and the work of the Holy Spirit helping my infirmities; and my soul springs once more to the battle with eager, devouring joy. Thus we find both the nature of the Beasts and the secret of their defeat. The Beasts of Ephesus are in every sinner's heart and in every soul's environment. There is no escape from them but in victory, in city or country, at home or abroad. They are the spirits of "the world, the flesh and the devil."

We thus have before us the general theme of the proposed series of articles. In these articles the class of persons which I especially wish to address is made up for the most part of young Christians. For the last seventeen years I have been brought, in the providence of God, into peculiar relations to this class of people and have learned not only to watch with peculiar interest their spiritual growth, but also to love them with a peculiar intensity, and to set a measureless value upon the hope, the energy, the generosity, the high aims and sublime possibilities of young men and young women just entered upon the Christian life. I shall not have to do with the vicious or dissipated, the prodigal or the courtesan, except indirectly. My present field is that of young church members. My motive is not simply to point out dangers, to utter warnings, or to keep Christian life from deteriorating; but also, and chiefly, to help young Christians to plant their feet on higher and safer ground; to inquire into the causes of spiritual inefficiency, and lead my readers into the secret of heroic and joy-bringing service. I shall assume, therefore, that those whom I address are in sympathy with me and are ready to accept such suggestions and arguments as may seem pertinent and reasonable.

My task, therefore, is the delightful one of speaking to those who already appreciate the motives that moved and swayed the soul of Paul in his conflict with the Beasts of Ephesus. Let it be distinctly understood, then, that in traversing the ground of the proposed articles the principle advocated is not simply that of self denial. The secret of Christian victory is not repression, but inspiration. We kill the devil by awakening the angel in the soul. We are not to fight the good fight all our days on the low line of the defensive. The heroic saints of God go out to victory and joy aggressively, along the line of positive virtue. They set out with the conviction that the world is not to be avoided, but conquered and subdued. With this fact in view, two things become absolutely necessary:

1. *A fixed spiritual purpose.* Carlyle once asked an Edinburgh student what he was studying for. The young man said he had not made up his mind. "The man without a purpose," said Carlyle, "is like a ship without a rudder; a waif, a nothing, a no-man. Have a purpose in life, if it is only to kill and divide and sell oxen well. But have a purpose, and having it, throw such strength of mind and muscle into your work as God has given you." But Carlyle's

rugged language falls short of the exquisite touch and force of that of the Apostle James, who says, "He that wavereth is like a surge of the sea, driven of the wind and tossed." Where can you find anything so absolutely the thing of circumstances as a wave of the sea? Its very existence is due to the wind. It rises or falls, is fierce or gentle, high or low, is rolled or tossed, in this direction or that, absolutely at the whim of the breeze, and when the wind ceases the wave is gone also. So is a man without a fixed spiritual purpose. If good influences surround him, he will be good or goodish. If evil influences come, he will be evil. If public opinion is favorable to religion, he will be religious; if adverse, he will be non-committal. If the Beasts of Ephesus are fierce and aggressive, he will decide that they are too strong to be overcome; if they are tame and gentle and winning, he will lie down with them in their den.

On the other hand, a fixed spiritual purpose to go forth and conquer the world, within and without, for Christ, will make man the master of his circumstances. And one of the grandest facts of our nature is that, even in this world of low ideals and false maxims and models, every young Christian can, if he will, go like Paul into the noise and glare of a godless city, into the rush of trade, into the crowded street, into the great congregation where false lights flame and low standards and wrong principles prevail, and yet be alone with his own great purpose; alone with his sublime faith amid the faithless; alone with God amid the godless and the vile.

2. Along with this fixed spiritual purpose every soul needs a *settled Christian policy.* The purpose answers the question, Shall I be a Christian at all? The settled policy decides what kind of a Christian I shall be. This policy

should not be left to be settled by circumstances as they arise, but should be settled, as far as possible, in advance. There are many questions of casuistry, or morality, or expediency, some of them in the church and some between the church and the world, which every Christian has to meet, and the settlement of which determines what kind of Christian one is going to be in the world. I do not urge a rash or hasty decision, but a wise and deliberate one, as to what attitude you will take toward certain questions which are in controversy, certain amusements, certain lines of business, certain phases of public sentiment and fashion, certain practices of society. Each one must settle these questions ultimately for himself. And he must do it in view of all the light he can get, as to their bearing on his own life, the life of his friends, the cause of Christ, and upon his own supreme spiritual purpose. Outside authority or restrictive rule cannot settle any but plain facts of revelation or self-evident truths. What each Christian needs is an intelligent reason of his own for his chosen policy, formed in view of his fundamental purpose to live for the glory of God. It is on this account that we urge a settled Christian policy, that every Christian should, as far as possible, take up these practical questions of life and decide what attitude he will take regarding them, on principle, and in advance, before the soul's environment takes final shape and crowds them upon him in the form of temptations. No Christian is in a proper condition to settle a doubtful question of casuistry or self-indulgence after he is strongly tempted to follow a certain Course. It is leaving these questions unsettled as to what attitude they will take, until they are forced upon the will for immediate action in the form of temptation, that gives the Beasts advantage and robs the church of its spiritual power. It can never be a matter of indifference what attitude we take toward the Beasts of Ephesus, which meet us at every turn. It is safe to say with Dr. Bushnell that, "It is not conformity we want. It is not being able to beat the world in its own way, but it is to stand apart, and above the world, and produce the impression of a holy and separated life. This only can give us true Christian power."

In conclusion, it may be said, that the utter inexperience of multitudes of young Christians when they leave the home and go out into the world is reason enough why Christian ministers should not only hold but teach sound principles and rules with regard to the kind of beasts their tender flock may expect to meet. I cannot agree with the sentiment of an excellent friend who says that "everything is gained and nothing lost, by remanding to the back seat all discussion of amusements which are not sinful *per se.*" Paul did not confine his instructions to practices which were sinful *per se*. He laid down great guiding Christian principles in addition to those of moral science, which will always be the safe guard of the church.

The question, What is sinful or righteous *per se*? is not the one which meets young Christians most frequently. The question of absolute right and wrong has become largely a matter of civil law in Christian nations. It is the question of what is *best* for the soul and best for the cause of Christ, which the Christian stands for in the world. It is on these questions that the inexperienced Christian needs instruction. It would be foolish to say that a pastor should not speak of the dangerous tendency of the modern theater because the act of attending the theater is not a sin *per se*.

Many an unsuspecting soul has stumbled into limbo

over this talk about "*per se.*" It is the *tendency* of things not necessarily sinful *per se* that needs a clear light. Of course the great motives that gave Paul his victory—inspiration rather than repression, "the expulsive power of a new affection"—will be the pastor's ground of appeal. But after all he is bound to send forth the young souls instructed as to the nature of the Beasts to be fought, as well as the secret of victory.

Chapter II:
The Young Christian
and the City

THE RELATION of the city to Christian life and power is growing every day more important. The modern city of Christendom differs from the ancient pagan city in this: That in addition to its innumerable perils to the spiritual life, it also has a few great advantages. While it presents the worst temptations, it also furnishes the greatest motives to self-denial and the grandest opportunities for service. It is the place where some of the best forces of our civilization gather; but also where the worst elements of wrecked humanity overwhelmingly concentrate. Aside from a small minority of Christian homes and a few Christian churches, standing like lonely beacon lights, illuminating a little space, it is by no means certain that the great modern city is much better than the ancient. New York, Cincinnati or Chicago is as truly a city of "many adversaries " as was ancient Ephesus; and the forces that antagonize the new life are probably not reduced.

The chief fruits of Christianity thus far appear in the individual, not in the city, as a whole. The church and the city are constantly acting and reacting upon each other, and the natural tendency is to find a common level. The result is, Christianity is not always really Christian. It is taking care of itself. Its attitude is not Apostolic. Its policy is timid, its pulse beats feebly and its voice is thin and low, as compared with the rampant roaring spirit of the city.

There the fact of bad government, of low political standards, of party zeal at the expense of party virtue, and the selfish use of money especially prevail.

Ex-President White of Cornell University says, "Without the slightest exaggeration, we may assert that with very few exceptions the city governments of the United States are the worst in Christendom; the most expensive, the most inefficient, the most corrupt." There the courts are corrupted and injustice is meted out by juries of saloon-keepers and thugs. There sensational and corrupting literature is especially accessible to the young. There the new curse of the Sunday secular paper is thrust in every Christian's face. There the glaring advertisements of vice, the obscene pictures of prostituted art meet the young Christian's eye unsought. There is the Sunday theater with its Satanic effrontery, reminding the Christian of his dishonored Christ and his lost Sabbath. There stands the brothel, luring men and women together to the portals of hell. There, as the cause and home of almost every other vice, "the distinct and mighty school of self indulgence," despiritualizing men's minds and breaking down all the bulwarks of moral rectitude and self-control, stands the saloon, open day and night. And there, worst of all, the great busy, hurrying world of pleasure-seeking and gain-getting is acquiescing in the existence of the saloon as it does in the existence of the church, and getting bravely accustomed to the woe and wickedness of the one, as it does to the high aims of the other. There, also, multitudes of well-to-do people who wear the Christian name, go cheerfully about their secular business in the presence of unspeakable want and misery, on the one hand, and measureless wealth and luxury on the other, as if all this were the arrangement of God!

The peculiar sins of the great commercial centers of today are just as real as those of Ephesus or Rome. One might almost think the Apostle was describing in his apocalyptic vision, a modern Babylon, rather than the ancient, when he speaks of the "traffic in merchandise of gold and silver, and precious stones, and pearls, and fine linen, and purple, and silk, and scarlet, and all thine wood, and every vessel of ivory and every vessel made of most precious wood, brass and iron and marble, and cinnamon, and spice, and incense and ointment, and frankincense, and wine, and oil, and flour and wheat, and cattle, and sheep, and merchandise of horses and chariots, and slaves, AND THE SOULS OF MEN."

Here, then, are the Beasts of the modern Ephesus, with which young disciples of Christ have to contend. And when we reflect that 290 out of every thousand of our population live in cities, great and small; that one in every five in this country live in cities of 50,000 or upward; that in the last forty years the population of the fifty principal cities has increased six fold, while that of the whole country has increased only three fold; that in every corner of the land the rush is toward a still greater congestion of population at such points; and therefore that vast numbers of young Christians just entering upon life either do or inevitably will spend their days in cities and have to meet such forces of evil—I say when we think of this, the question becomes imperious, "What is to be the type of the spiritual life of the future? What is to be the history of the church of God in America? What shall we do in the presence of these Beasts of Ephesus? Shall we fight or shall we surrender?" Our salvation and that of our country depends upon the answer.

The influence of great pities is not confined to their own limits. It affects the religious faith and life of the State and Nation; nay, it reaches even to the ends of the earth.

The result of this low state of spiritual life is painfully manifest. To a looker-on in most of our great cities, the first impression is that the churches are located where they are least needed, and that they are far too few for the population. In Boston there is one church to 1,600 people; in New York, one to 2,300; in St. Louis, one to 2,800; in Chicago, one to 2,300. In a single district of the latter city, says one of its own daily journals, there is a population of 50,000 with Sunday-school accommodations for 2,000. "It is full of theaters, saloons and gambling dens." "The churches," it is said, "don't care for that district. They are looking after the avenues "—what they seem to want is millions of money, not millions of men. In one section of New York City we are told there are 360,000 people, with one saloon to every 118 persons and one Protestant church to every 11,624 persons.

Now the reason for this state of things is largely a social one. It cannot be denied that the spirit of the world has entered too much into the heart of the church, excluding from it the spirit of the Cross; blinding its eyes to the agony and despair of the "submerged tenth," deafening its ears to the Macedonian cry from the other part of the city, and tempting it to seek first the kingdom of creature comforts and the money to buy them. It is painfully evident that the vast multitude of churches are identified with the well-to-do and well-dressed portion of humanity and widely separated from the larger part of God's toiling poor. This has an ugly look. It does not suggest the Apostolic

Church. It does not bring to mind the Christ. It does not suggest the Golden Rule. The very fact of the establishment of so-called "people's churches" is an acknowledgement that some of the existing churches certainly have not been regarded as "people's churches."

In saying these things, we do not forget that there are many noble efforts being made by the churches, many grand agencies employed, many consecrated souls at work for humanity in our great cities. There is the work of the city missionary societies, the agencies of the Woman's Christian Temperance Union, the children's aid societies, homes for newsboys, etc. All these show what Christianity can do, but how meager, how inadequate, compared with the measureless need of the past and the latent power of the churches.

Now my appeal is to young Christians to rise up in their strength and convert all churches into "people's churches." I speak to young men, and to young women too, "because they are strong." What I would fain say to them, if they would listen, is that they must fight the Beasts of Ephesus not only outside, but in the Church of Christ. A new type of religion, with broader views of the meaning of the Cross, and a more Pauline consecration, must permeate the church, if the world is to be saved. There must be a more aggressive type of church life. We must start out with the conviction that we have joined not simply a divine Being but also a divine cause. To the young, the progressive, the heroic, in the church of today, Christ himself makes this appeal. Nothing in Scripture is more touching than the Savior's sympathy and solicitude for *Christians*. Our solicitude for a man often ceases when we see him received into the church. Not so with Christ.

Even when the shadow of the cross was falling upon his own life, his supreme thought and care was for the well-being, the efficiency of Christians, who were to be the light of the world, the saving element in society. "I am no more in the world; but these are in the world." I shall still work for the world but it must be henceforth through "these," and upon what kind of Christians they shall be will depend the kind of church the world is to have and so the destiny of the race. They are "in the world," and so tempted to live on the world's plane, to use the world's tactics, to lose sight of their sublime mission, to turn a deaf ear to the pathetic, perpetual, inarticulate cry of the world's need. "These are in the world," and to be in it, to meet its pains and storms, its allurements, its curse and its falsehood, "*Holy Father, keep them!*"

This is the Savior's solicitude today.

Two things, therefore, I would ask young Christians to consider: First the vastness of the *opportunity;* second, the grandeur of the motive. The city itself opens a door to every dweller therein for Christian service which cannot elsewhere be found. More can be done for Christ and humanity in a given time, and with smaller proportionate outlay of money, in the great city than anywhere else on the globe. Everything is within reach. There is the appeal of ignorance and suffering and want. There at the Christian's door is the hunger and thirst and temptation and pain and sadness and sin of our dilapidated humanity, lying in its moral misery under the face of God, struggling not for character or culture or style, but for bare existence. And there, in the Christian's hands, are the glad tidings of great joy for all people, if they only have the heart to utter them. All lands are full today of great cities lifting up their cry for the good news. This was the "great and effectual door" which Paul found opened and which led him to devote his life to the great cities of the Roman Empire.

The motive which Paul found not only sufficient, but over-mastering, was the fact of *immortality*, the infinite destiny of every man, the assurance of eternal life with God. From this fact spring all worthy conceptions of humanity. With the hope of immortality gone, the value of the soul ceases, and men are not worth living for. If there were nothing beyond this life of sin and suffering and tears, the motive for heroic self-mastery and service would be gone. If we believed that we were to die like the beasts, we should soon begin to live like the beasts. If a man is to die like a dog, why should he live like an angel? No; the inspiring motives which thrilled the souls of prophets and apostles are all included in Christ's conception of man, his moral freedom, his accountability, his immortality, his capacity to live with and be like God. We can thus see what Christ has done for the world. He has set on foot a divine upward movement in the life of humanity which is to touch and inspire every people under heaven. He has supplied us all with the infinite motives which impel to love-service and to victory.

Oh, that young men and women of today, whose souls have been touched by the Spirit of God, might also be heart-smitten as Paul was with this great conquering motive! Oh, that they, when tempted to acquiesce in things as they are, when solicited to go with the crowd, to simply eat and drink and die, might catch the inspiration of immortality! Oh, that every reader might think of the throne of judgment and the glory of the self-denying Christ, and so fling himself into the battle!

Chapter III:
The Young Christian
and Money

1. LET NO reader suppose that I am going to denounce the possession of wealth or the proper accumulation of the same. Would that we were all rich and all in the line of making more. Virtue does not consist in poverty, or in incapacity to accumulate. Neither does it consist in acquisitiveness. The strong Biblical attitude on this subject is simply against making acquisition of money a master passion. There is a difference between living to eat and eating to live. There is a whole hemisphere of difference between making money to live and living to make money; between possessing wealth and letting wealth possess us. It is the latter which the Apostle says "pierces men through with many sorrows and drowns then in destruction and perdition," and the poor are just as really exposed to that method of "taking off " as the rich.

Money, like brains, is not an evil, but a good. The danger, like that of fire, lies not in its use but in its abuse, and it is probable that no man ever makes a wrong use of his money till he has first made a wrong use of himself. Money is the tool of mind as really as is a crowbar or a fountain-pen. Mind ought not to be the tool of money. "Money is power," because it secures a great many things that all souls desire. Its relation to human desires, together with its abundance in this country, makes it a giant power for both good and evil in the hands of a half-Christianized civilization. Fifty billions of wealth in the nation; ten billions of it in the hands of evangelical Christians, and that increasing at the rate of six hundred thousand per day; increasing, that is, seventy-one times faster than our gifts to all home and foreign missions increase; that is a state of things which fires the imagination of old and young. For money is a power which not only gratifies but creates human desires. The desire of the saint for the promotion of God's kingdom, and of the worldling for the gratification of selfishness, are both stimulated by this servant alike of good and evil, who works for all without respect of persons. This is where the danger of money lies. It has always had this power in all ages, nations and climes.

2. It is for this reason that Christ and the apostles uttered their warnings against the danger of riches. Money affords the most subtle and universal temptation to which Christians are exposed. This is especially true in cities, where the various objects of desire are forced upon the attention in a way to inflame the lust of the eye and the pride of life. Who has not seen many a character which seemed to start out well in the Christian life, wilt and die, like a tender plant when a worm is at its root? Who has not seen Christians who could date their apostasy from Christ to a particular time when the money god bought their souls for some petty gratification of the flesh? "What multitudes of fresh, manly young fellows," says President Gates, "the high aspirations of home and college still radiant on their faces, we have seen each year sucked down into the outer circles of the great whirlpools of speculation in our cities." What follies and crimes and consequent soul-wrecks we have all seen as the result of this one passion. The false words, the frauds, the thefts, the

defalcations, the murders, the worse than murder of the opium traffic in poor China and the rum traffic in Darkest Africa, are all the horrid offspring of this master passion for money, or what money will buy. The daily papers reek with the accounts of the collapses of character in the church and in the world among rich and poor alike, in business firms, and national political committees, where men have sold themselves for money.

Among Christian young people who seldom, perhaps, go to the length of defalcation, the temptation takes the form of small self-indulgences. The sin of getting and hoarding is less frequent among the young than the sin of waste and misappropriation. The cigar, the occasional glass of wine, the late supper, the questionable entertainment, the candy habit, all cost money which as Christians we owe to God. The result of these things is that when a call comes to help the cause of Christ we have nothing to give. We break our covenant with God to gratify the flesh. The heart learns to lust for display, elegance, luxury, competition in style of dress. Money is the one thing that gratifies and at the same time stimulates and multiplies all of these desires. The power which money possesses tempts men to live beyond their means; to keep up a scale of expenditure requiring an income of three thousand dollars a year when the real income is only two thousand. Then follows the desperate struggle to make up the deficit: speculation, fraud, stealing, gambling, forgery, dishonest failures; to all of these methods does the self-indulgent soul resort. An English assignee in bankruptcy says he found that out of seventy-six cases, forty-nine bankrupts were ruined by simply living beyond their means. During the last few months a young man, a member of one of the New York churches, a worker in Sunday-school and Christian Endeavor Society, has fallen into this snare, and is now in the penitentiary.

While in the tombs he wrote his pastor the story of his down-fall. He says, "In 1888, notwithstanding a good salary, I lived up my income and contracted some debts by easy living, at theater, in society and in the membership of organizations I ought not to have joined on account of financial inability to do so. Several creditors were pressing me continually, and having drawn ahead at the store, I did not know which way to turn. One day, Satan showed me the way out." Then follows the account of a long series of deliberate frauds upon his employer, each of which he hoped to make right before it should be discovered, till he was involved to the amount of $5,000. As the cords tightened about him, he began to lie to his widowed mother. He took her plate and jewelry under pretense of putting them in safe deposit; and pawned them. Later he took her ring and watch and pawned them also. Last of all he forged his pastor's name to a check on the bank. At last he was detected, fled, was pursued, and for days was in such agony that he longed to be arrested, and at last he was. He was not a gambler, or a debauchee; but loved what money would secure and so lived beyond his means and "Satan showed him the way out."

The dreadful thing about the love of money is that even when it never breaks out into open vice and public disgrace, it does lower the spiritual tone of the church and the community. It kills the spirit of self-denial, dries up the streams of benevolence, and so defeats the gospel of Christ.

3. Now God's safeguard for his children against this danger is divinely simple and beautiful. It is not to flee

from wealth or the accumulation of it but from its misappropriation. It is *first* to occupy the soul with God's thoughts; to steep the mind in Christ's view of life, Christ's estimate of money, Christ's conception of manhood and womanhood. This is always within the power of the will. Be a man of God. Be God's man in the set of your purpose, the determination of your will. Then Paul's words will apply, "Thou, O man of God, flee these things. Follow after righteousness, faith, love, patience, meekness. Fight the good fight of faith. Lay hold of eternal life whereunto ye are called."

SECOND: Crucify the love of money by the love of Christ. Let the strong man who holds the palace be crowded out by the stronger than he. This, too, is within every Christian's power. That is, form at once the habit of systematic and large-hearted *giving*. Give your *idol* to Christ. Giving to self is the generic sin of mankind; giving to Christ is the generic virtue. The exercise of the one crucifies the other. There is no other way. Here we have God's sublime conception of life and salvation; that while we give to save the world, we ourselves are thereby saved from that danger which threatens to ruin both church and world at the same time.

This giving does not imply that God dictates in detail just how, or when, or what proportion we shall give. He has left all that for us to settle in the light of the general principles of the new life. He has laid upon us as his children the supreme honor and responsibility of this *free* stewardship of all we have and all that we can honestly get. He wants to cultivate thoughtfulness and conscientiousness. He is building character; men, not mechanism. He might dictate to each one just what he should do, and how much he should give; but that would make not men but machines. He throws us lovingly upon our character, puts us to the crucial test and leaves us to decide. This is essential to our Christian probation. This does not slacken the cords of our responsibility, but tightens them. A Christian cannot say, "This matter of how much I should give to the cause of Christ is left unsettled by the Bible and therefore I may put it at a low figure." The reverse is the fact. The less specific God's precepts are, the greater is the Christian's responsibility. A cashier in a bank to whose discretion is committed the whole charge of the business, would be far more responsible than the clerk who simply follows specific rules So here, in the building of Christian character, too much revelation would be just as bad as too little. To stimulate and fortify the conscientious habit of giving, God keeps before us the mighty appeal of the world's need. He says, There is the field. There are the souls for whom I died. In proportion as you love me, decide in the court of your own soul what you ought to do with the money over which I have made you stewards. It is mine, not yours, but I want you to have the honor and benefit of its distribution.

4. The wisdom and necessity of this method are clear when we reflect that,

(1.) A true unselfish spirit of *giving* is fundamental to Christian character. To become a giver rather than a receiver is a bottom principle of the gospel. It is the radical idea of the new life. There is nothing that lies so close to the very soul of the soul, or more deep down in the very elements of spiritual mindedness than the habitual exercise of giving; prayer itself is not more fundamental to character. The amount we are able to give is of secondary importance. The great thing is to be radically in the spirit and process of giving to God. This is the highest test of conversion. There is probably no other absolute test of whether the dominion of selfishness is broken and the dominion of love established in the soul. Make the experiment purely for Christ's sake of giving away what you have been accustomed to lavish on yourself, and you will find that nothing goes so straight to the center and soul of your being, either as a warning or as a joy, as that.

(2.) This spirit of giving is the thing above all others that makes men like *God*. Bear in mind that the leading fact in the revelation of God is that he is a great giver. Almost all that we know of God is that he is "an infinite giver. From this fact the apostle inferred his nature: "God is Love." "This is the highest conception we can form of any being, that he should find a conscious blessedness in giving without limit and without exhaustion forevermore." And it is clear that one thing which makes a man like God is to become an unselfish giver. We talk about imitating Christ and walking in his likeness, and we can do neither till we become *givers*. We yearn for the joy of the Lord; but the infinitely holy joy of God lies in his giving. The divine likeness does not depend upon the amount of money or time or talent given, but the *spirit*. Without that, all so-called religion is a dry, dead, impudent parade.

(3.) Thus only shall we escape what the apostle regards as underlying all other sins: the " love of money;" that love which makes gain rather than God the chief end of existence. The moral discipline of giving is one of our supreme blessings. It is a refining and sanctifying force in the new life. To talk about being sanctified without this Godlike spirit is sheer delusion. "For they that *will* be rich fall into temptation and a snare and into many foolish and hurtful lusts, which drown men in destruction and perdition."

To the Christian young woman then, let me say, the chief value of money , to a woman is not in the clothes that it will buy. Are you from a home of wealth? Then you can afford to dress plainly and have an abundance to give to God's cause. You can set the much-needed example of plainness of dress in the house of God, which would do more toward winning back the love of the poor to the Church of Christ than anything else you can do. But if you have not wealth back of the elegance of your dress, you are either wronging a hardworking father or you are cheating yourself out of the blessing of giving liberally of your own earnings. How terrible it would be to hear, instead of those sweet words, "She hath done what she could," these: "She spent so much on herself that she could not do anything for me."

To the Christian young man let me say this: If financial ambition is growing upon you and tempting you to tricks of trade, strangle it, or it will strangle your soul. Live frugally. Make simplicity, economy, and self-denying love daily companions. Expend, only as you have the means. Reckon only on what is actually yours. It is not well to count on something miraculous turning up. You cannot live on air, much less on credit. Rest on your own hard money though it be but a penny. To borrow when you know you cannot pay is stealing. A tender conscience maybe an expensive luxury in these days, but when God's test of manhood is applied, it will be health to your countenance and marrow to your bones.

Chapter IV:
The Young Christian and Bad Books

WHEN occasionally we are startled by the fall of a Christian character, the blame is not all with the fallen. There are a thousand influences, which, though never exonerating the criminal, do facilitate and encourage the crime. The moral atmosphere; the habits and standards of society; the mad rush of everybody for wealth; the false theories of political economy; the immoral views of "cut-throat" competition and the survival of the fittest; the villainous custom of denouncing bad men in theory and voting for them in practice; knocking scoundrels down in the church and holding them up at the polls; all these arc partakers of the crime through which the man fell.

Among the malign influences which help young people downward, there is probably none more subtle or powerful than that of bad literature. The influence of books, as such, upon human character, for both weal and woe, is probably the most potent force of these times.

A recent writer tells us that, while visiting the State prison of Indiana, the chaplain of that institution informed him that out of 121 prisoners then under his care, and who were convicted before they came of age, ninety-two attributed their crimes to the fact that their minds were corrupted and poisoned by reading the vile and false papers and books that are everywhere flooding the land today.

"Of all the things which man can do or make here

below," says Carlyle, "by far the most momentous and wonderful and worthy, are the things we call books." "Books," says Milton, "are not dead things, but do contain a potency of life in them to be as active as the soul was whose progeny they are; nay, they do preserve as in a vial the purest efficacy and ex traction of the living intellect that bred them." Oral address will always have its place and power, but it touches only thousands while the printed page reaches its tens of thousands. Today books are practically omnipresent and omnipotent. They are cheap and overwhelmingly abundant; 25,000 new volumes are issued" every year. Many of them are good, and how many of them are worse than worthless God only knows. At any rate they are read, and no friend of humanity can be indifferent to the influence of that reading on the destiny of souls and the kingdom of God. It would be a delightful task to contemplate the influence of good books upon the human soul; but our present business is to look specially in the other direction,

One of the Beasts of our modern Ephesus with which young Christians especially have to fight, nay, perhaps I might say a whole menagerie of them under a single name, is *bad literature*. The world is so full of books that, as Arthur Helps has said, " It is like standing in an orchard laden with fruit. It is not so much a matter of choice, as a matter of falling to and taking the best. The worm-eaten and wind-blasted and rotten will of course be passed by." But the trouble lies precisely there: the "worm-eaten and wind-blasted and rotten" are not passed by. They are the cheapest and most accessible, and hungry boys and girls do not stop to discriminate. It is to be feared that even parents are not sufficiently awake to the danger from this source. "Many are alive to the danger of bad associates, who are quite insensible to the danger of bad books." The fascination of bad books is more dangerous than that of bad men. Indeed, as Victor Hugo says, "The book is the man in his moral or immoral essence." It can be smuggled into the home and taken to a boy's room when its author would be shut out of doors.

There are several classes and degrees of bad literature, looked at from the Christian point of view.

First. The dignified and respectable atheistic or infidel books, written with great literary skill and power, and containing valuable information, but written by men who despise God and hate religion. Gibbon's Rome and Hume's England are of this class. "Of the tens of thousands who have read Gibbon's History of Rome for historical purposes," says ex-President Porter, "few have been able to escape the *indirect* influence which pervades it in every part, as the seeds of death will shake themselves from the gorgeous robe of damask and gold that has been worn by one smitten with the plague." Men of well-established Christian principles may consult such books with safety and profit; but not so the young Christian whose mind lies open to all the foul winds that blow. And, happily for our times, there is no need of going to such sources for historical information.

There is a second class of books which may be called semi-religious. Professedly fair, but ethically false, they claim to have the religious interests of humanity at heart, and yet pander to unworthy motives by a subtle indirection. They are written by people who have discovered a weak spot in human nature, and propose to make money and fame for themselves by its quack treatment. Like the

Platonic philosophy, they teach one to seek, but not to find; to struggle, but not to rest. Their characteristic effect is *fever*. What do they contain? A dream with a sad waking; a fling at quiet life to make the book smart; a sneer or two at simple, old-fashioned gospel religion, to make it sell. What is the result? The result is like that of the little book mentioned in the tenth chapter of the Apocalypse.

But the third class of bad reading is that composed of the openly and positively immoral books, and especially *pictorial* publications, with which every town is flooded; that class of low fiction which deals with the lives of pirates, thieves and foot pads, like Beadle's Dime Novels, the very titles and pictures of which are a curse to boys and girls. There are also numberless cheap illustrated papers and magazines like the "Police Gazette" which make no pretense to anything but a desire for money through appeals to the lowest and worst in humanity. They are simply made to sell, and they do sell. This is the food that thousands of boys are feeding upon, some of them members of the Church of Christ! And this is only a single degree worse than the love-sick twaddle, called fiction, of which thousands of girls are wasting both time and womanhood.

In that remarkable book called "Letters from Hell," recommended by George McDonald, a man is represented as writing warning letters to a friend, from the infernal pit. Speaking of books, he says, "Whatever is bad of course comes here to Hell. And so of printed matter, whatever is mortally evil or arrogantly stupid tends hitherward; the books arriving first, then the authors follow, and then the publishers come along with them. Polite literature has furnished us many books, very popular here, though often immodest. They are represented by two classes: the purely sensational and the sensationally impure; the former being content to hint where the latter touch boldly; the one supremely worthless, the other wickedly ingenious." But it is little comfort that such books "go to their own place" after the mischief is done.

Now the young Christian must understand that he cannot read or see such stuff, even out of curiosity, without destroying the enamel of his character. He will gradually lower the tone of his moral feelings, till at last the resisting power of the soul is gone; and when temptation comes he will fall. Of course there is a type of literature of a still deeper depth of depravity than what I have alluded to, though it is doubtful if it can be any more destructive. That, however, as I am speaking to Christians, is not only not to be read, but " not to be once mentioned among you, as becometh saints." The result of reading such literature is, first, a waste of time; second, a destruction of the moral sense; third, pollution of the imagination; fourth, ruin of wholesome taste for good reading, and, fifth, a distaste for the Bible, which makes practical religion impossible.

Now I shall not undertake in this article to recommend a list of books. My chief object now is to suggest a few simple principles.

1. No sincere Christian can afford to spend time on a *frivolous* book. It is no defense of a book to say, " It is harmless." The world is in such perishing need of strong, consecrated souls, and there are so many great themes demanding attention and fitted to undergird the soul for high duty, that no being made in the image of God and redeemed by the blood of Christ has any right to read a book simply because it is harmless, or simply to please

himself , or to kill time. If one reads to kill time he will kill something more valuable than time. "It is as low and immoral to read as it is to eat, simply to please the palate."

2. What should Christians do about reading infidel books?

First, Keep them away from children and beginners in the new life. The physical system of a full-grown man may bear a degree of poison that would kill a child. The first time a child uses edged tools he cuts his fingers, but the day may come when he can use them to great advantage.

Secondly, Discriminate among infidel books, There are moral and immoral unbelievers. There are men who write against Christianity because they hate it. They are prejudiced in mind and therefore illogical in argument. Such books are not fit to be read anywhere. But there are books written by honest doubters which may sometimes help a mature and candid Christian to see the weak points of his own faith and may help him to help his fellow men. No man should refuse to listen to a fair and candid presentation of all the objections to his own religion. But he should never read a work of an infidel without conscientiously reading at the same time the best defense of his own faith that he can find. Many a Christian innocently reads a skeptical book through and through because it is fresh, startling, and breezy, who never read a standard work on Christian evidence in his life and perhaps does not propose to.

Thirdly, The Christian's motive in reading such books must be the better to honor God. No Christian can consistently read a book hostile to his faith from mere curiosity Indeed he cannot consistently read even a good book from mere curiosity, much less a book that strikes directly at

Christ. If a child of God goes into a saloon or a brothel it must be to save somebody as Christ would do; to lift the fallen or expose the sin. That is a very serious business and the same principle applies in the matter of reading doubtful books.

3. What are we to do about devotional reading? It is certainly not wise to neglect it. Our spiritual nature is quite as susceptible of improvement and inspiration from books as our intellectual. The most efficient Christians of every age owe much of their power to religious reading. If, as young Christians, we have no relish at first for devotional books, we are not to be discouraged. It can be cultivated. Besides, a true young Christian is not the person to be governed by silly likes or dislikes; but rather by his great spiritual needs. We need to keep in mind that the true aim of devotional reading is a double one; to secure strong convictions and deep, holy emotions. The former is the foundation of the latter. Therefore, when we sit down to read a religious book it is no child's play. It is to be done with no less seriousness and conscientiousness than the entering upon public worship or going into our closet to pray.

4. What about Sunday reading in particular? Whatever else the Christian may read, it is certain that he cannot afford to spend Sunday reading on that latest device of the Devil to make money at the expense of Christian character: the Sunday *secular paper.* Apart from the work of Sabbath desecration in publishing and distributing them, the worse influence of Sunday papers is on the readers themselves. It is not possible for any Christian family to form the habit of spending the Sabbath hours over the average Sunday paper without spiritual deterioration.

Here, for example, is the advertised list of attractions in an issue of the Sunday Cleveland *Leader*. The following list was advertised Saturday afternoon to create a demand for the Sunday issue: "In the serial story, Mrs. Stephens will relate the adventures of Dick Shelton and the outlaws; Edward Everett Hale will give the second of his talks on the tariff; Mrs. Wakeman will write about coffee plantations around Trinidad; Mrs. Sherwood has a charming article on summer life in the country; a number of experts will tell how to play tennis; Jennie June will give valuable hints to young women on dress making; Ed Mott will give another story on hunting in which he relates the experience of an old panther-hunter who lived all his life in the woods."

Now, aside from the impudent pretense of furnishing these papers to do the community good, a pretense which every intelligent person treats with contempt, it is plain that the weak point in Christian life lies just here, in Christian people buying, paying for, and sitting down to sully the hours of the Lord's day and debauch their spiritual life with such vapid and despiritualizing stuff as the above. It is not strange that companies or corporations which have no religion and no God but mammon should try to add to their income by furnishing such Sunday feasts. But that so many professed disciples of the Lord Jesus should fall into this Satanic trap with their eyes open, and should train their children in this mischievous form of Sabbath desecration, is a scandal to the whole Church of God. The religious life can no more endure it without decay than the body can endure the malaria of the valley of the Maumee.

Sunday should neither be a day of mental drudgery nor mental dissipation. "Every reader should make a business and conscience of having his Sunday reading intellectually strong as well as spiritually devout." Sunday should be a day for the girding up of the higher life for the conflicts and cares of the week. A Christian who does not find himself on Monday morning better fitted to meet the temptations to worldliness and meanness, than he was before, has probably abused God's gift of the Sabbath.

In your reading don't feed simply on the publications of today. Get the wisdom of past ages which has stood the test of time. Don't read too many books. Hobbes once said, "If I read as many books as numbers of other do, I should be as ignorant as they." Have a high purpose in all of your reading. Select the history, the biography, the poetry, the novels that are true and strong and pure, the religious thoughts that will counteract the narrowing and crowding influence of your daily life. Cultivate the habit of reading aloud at home.

Chapter V:
The Young Christian
and the Theater

IN discussing the subject of the theater, it is necessary to limit and define the theme. It is not the subject of amusements. It is not whether it is ever right or wise to patronize the theater, It is not the subject of the drama as a department of literature. It is quite essential to clear ideas here, to distinguish between the drama as a literature, and the theater as a place of dramatic representation. It is never inconsistent to admire, profit by and praise the literature of Aechylus and Sophocles, in that noblest period of the great men of Greece, and yet abhor and condemn the Grecian stage. Neither is it difficult to draw a line between the peerless dramas of Shakespeare and the theater of today. What we are now concerned with is the theater. In the interest of brevity and clearness, it is necessary to limit still farther. Our theme is *the influence of the theater upon morals and religion, as found in the history of the past and the observation of today.*

It is a remarkable fact that the ponderous treatise on the drama of all ages and nations, found in the Encyclopedia Britannica, does not touch the question of the influence of the theater upon moral character. The same may be said of the most of our books on the History of English Literature, though the winged and barbed words and disdainful style of Taine imply that from which virtue shrinks. The aim of such writers is to give the origin and development of the drama, and not to look at it, or the theater, from the moralist's point of view. We need, therefore, to go to philosophy and to general history for testimony on this point. The attitude which any one shall take in regard to the theater is not to be settled by law or by church authorities, or by art critics. It can only be settled by individuals, each one for himself, in view of facts and tendencies exhibited in history. It must also be understood here, that it is not an ideal theater, but the theater as it has been and is that we are to discuss. The ideal theater is an ideal *idea*. History can make no declaration in regard to what never existed.

I. What then is the verdict of history as to the moral influence of the theater? Among ancient Greek and Roman writers may be placed Plutarch, Xenophon, Plato, Socrates, Solon, Seneca, Tacitus, Ovid, and many others who have condemned the theater as hostile to public and private morals. "An English writer in the time of Charles the First," says Dr. Herrick Johnson, " made a catalogue of authorities against the stage, which contains almost every name of eminence in the heathen and Christian world." Plutarch condemned it at Athens as demoralizing the people, getting their money, corrupting their youth; and when the stage censorship failed to improve the plays the theater was suppressed by law. The Lacedaemonians would not tolerate it in any form. Grote, referring to the corrupting influences of Aristophanes, says that Greek comedy was degrading to the Athenian mind, and that Solon condemned it in the sixth century, B. C, as "a vicious novelty tending to corrupt the integrity of human dealings." Plato says: "Plays raise the passions and pervert the use of them, and of consequence are dangerous to morality." Uhlhorn, speaking of the theater in the Roman Empire, says:

"The adventures of deceived husbands, adulteries and amorous intrigues formed the staple of the plots. Virtue was made a mock of; the gods scoffed at, and everything worthy of veneration was dragged in the mire." Dr. Lord, in his "Old Roman World," takes the same ground. Philip Schaff says:

"The Roman theater became more and more the nursery of vice and deserved to be abhorred by all men of decent feeling and refined taste."[1] When Herod introduced the theater into Jerusalem, Josephus (not a Christian) denounced it as corrupting the morals of the Jewish nation. It was not surprising, therefore, that when Christianity appeared, the earliest Christians and the church fathers presented a united front against the theater.

Turning now to the "moral" and "miracle plays" of the Middle Ages, when Roman monks stupidly tried to utilize the stage in the interest of the church, it is evident that the attempt was a failure. The tendency of the crude

---

1 Sometimes a pagan utters sentiments which Christian ministers would do well to teach. Julian, the Apostate, when striving to re-establish Roman heathenism on the ruins of the Christian Church, stole from Christianity the following, which he deemed necessary to even a respectable and successful pagan religion: 11 The priest of the gods should never be seen in theaters or taverns. His conversation should lie chaste, his diet temperate, his friends of honorable reputation; and if he sometimes visits the Forum or the Palace, he should appear only as the advocate of those who have vainly solicited either justice or mercy. His studies should be suited to the sanctity of his profession. Licentious tales or comedies, or satires must be banished from his library, which ought solely to consist of historical and philosophical writings; of history which is founded in truth, and of philosophy which is connected with religion. The impious opinion of epicureans and sceptics deserve his abhorrence and contempt." (Gibbon's Rome. Vol. II, p. 426.

plays was against morality, rather than in favor of religion. The inevitable drift became more and more toward secularism, and the church had to abandon the effort and withdraw. Lecky says that after the thirteenth century these plays assumed a more popular form, their religious character speedily declined, and they "became at last one of the most powerful agents in bringing the church, and indeed religion, into disrepute." The history of the early English theater is comparatively well understood. Some of the first dramatic writers of note, such as Greene and Marlowe, were utterly dissolute men. Of the former of these, Green, the historian, says: "He was a drunkard and a roysterer, with whom hell and the after world were butts of ceaseless mockery." Marlowe was a skeptic, and died "in a shameful brawl."

Some of the first theaters of London were simply cockpits, where the lowest class of society carried on their revolting sport of cockfighting. One theater was actually called "The Cock-Pit," from which we still have the theatrical phrase, "The Pit." It is said than a young man once agreed to meet his friend at the door of the theater. In waiting a half hour for his friend, he was so impressed by the cries of the ushers, "This way to the pit! This way to the pit!" that, his Christian training getting the better of him, he concluded that he was on the brink of perdition and took to his heels. For a long time the theaters were attended only by men. The female parts of the drama were acted by young men and boys. No woman appeared on the stage until the time of the Restoration. The first part ever acted by a woman was that of Shakespeare's "Desdemona." This innovation was at first regarded as shocking and monstrous, even in that age, which Macaulay says, "were the days of servitude without loyalty, and sensuality without love; of dwarfish talents and gigantic vices; the paradise of cold hearts and narrow minds; the golden age of the coward, the bigot and the slave." It is certain that the entrance of woman upon the stage did not purify it. Some of the worst features of the Italian comedy were put upon the boards in England at this period. Of course the Puritans of England all along hated and fought the theater; and Mr. Green, the historian, says: "It was mainly the honest hatred of God-fearing men." Philip Sidney said, that by representing nothing but vice, the theater authorized the manners of debauched men and women. Macaulay tells us that "from the time the theaters were opened they became the seminaries of vice. Nothing charmed the depraved audience so much as to hear lines, grossly indecent, repeated by a beautiful girl supposed not yet to have lost her innocence." Sir Walter Scott, speaking of the theater of England and Scotland, even as late as his day, says; "It was abandoned to the vicious. The best portion of the house was set apart for abandoned characters." "The most refined theaters in the world," he says, "are destined to company so scandalous that persons not very nice in their taste of society must yet exclaim against the abuse." The charges against the theater in the city of London today are substantially what they were in the days of Charles the Second. The same has been true in America. Soon after the Declaration of Independence, Congress passed a resolution recommending to the several States the suppression of theatrical entertainments, as productive of "idleness, dissipation, and depravity of principles and manners."

Of the theaters of today, probably no one will deny that the vast majority are debased and debasing. They are the plague spots of our civilization. And even the most respectable and popular in our great cities, while they occasionally put upon the stage a clean drama to attract respectable people, are, for the most part, corrupt and corrupting. This is incontestably proved by the testimony even of the secular press. In New York City within fifteen years, the *Northern Monthly, The Round Table, The Nation, The Evening Post, The Tribune,* have all given evidence against the best theaters of that city, which ought to subject them to eternal infamy. The *Evening Post,* speaking of public sentiment, says: "There are many here who will welcome and enjoy a degree of licentiousness which would not be tolerated even in the English theater." The *Tribune* claims that Wallack's Theater "leads the van of the contemporary drama. When the season opens, a brilliant assemblage of character, mind, beauty and wit throngs its benches." "And this," says Dr. H. C. Haydn, "is what another paper says was put upon the boards at the opening night of Wallack's Theater for the entertainment of this brilliant assemblage. A *deodorized French farce* about the profligacy of married men and of some married women." There are certain plays acted there, which when first presented only men venture to witness. Then a few women go, blush and hang their heads, but in a few nights the whole is received with unveiled faces and "roars of laughter," by men and women alike. When a certain play, which I refuse to name, was brought on at Nibo's, says a secular paper, "very few men had the temerity to take women with them." The second evening, a small feminine element was present, but "before the second month city dames and carefully reared damsels ventured to gaze on the wanton dance and lewd tableaux. Even the 'demon dance' was soon received as a thing of course." "As a result," says the same paper, "the women have grown harder, ruder, less sensitive and modest." J. M. Buckley of New York, who made a candid study of no less than sixty plays, acted in the best theaters in that city, says: "If language which would not be tolerated among respectable people and would excite indignation if addressed to the most uncultivated servant girl by an ordinary young man, and profaneness which would brand him who uttered it as irreligious are improper amusements, then at least *fifty* of these plays are to be condemned. Of the other ten, with three or four exceptions, those which are morally unobjectionable are of a comparatively low order of execution." Within a few years the shocking facts were brought to light that in the most of the theaters of the great cities, as in the time of Sir Walter Scott, portions of the building were set apart for prostitutes and debauched men, and at one time in New York City such persons were admitted free; this last, however, is not true at the present time. A committee was once appointed to inquire into this feature of the case in the Royal Theater in London, and they reported that the theater could not be maintained if this class of persons were excluded. Dr. Haydn tells us that a similar committee reported in regard to Tremont Theater in Boston, that a part of the house was always frequented by this depraved class, and that it had always been so in every theater in Boston. A prominent theater in Philadelphia once advertised, as a great attraction to fashionable people, a play which had actually been condemned as too vile by the stage censors of Paris. I need not remind you that the terrible exposure of the Chicago theaters made by Dr. Herrick Johnson, a few years ago, was based largely upon the testimony of the dramatic critics connected with the secular papers of that city.

To any one who carefully examines the subject, the conclusion cannot be escaped that while the theater has afforded some amusement, some healthful, intellectual stimulus to a few, yet it has been like Gratiano's two grains of wheat in two bushels of chaff. History is against it, both as it has been and as it is. The best Christian sentiment of society at large has vastly improved, but the theater as a moral force is not better than in the days of the Restoration. I have recently sent out over eighty letters to prominent pastors in the chief cities of this country, asking among other things their judgment as to the effect of theater-going upon Christian life and usefulness. I have received between fifty and sixty replies. Six or eight of the writers take a negative position as to occasional attendance by Christians. Yet they say it is the exception and not the rule where theatergoers are active and spiritual minded. Two approve of the occasional attendance of Christians. All the rest believe in the expediency of absolute *total abstinence* for all good people, as the theater now is. And every man from whom I have heard, thinks that *habitual* or *indiscriminate* theater-going is a curse. I have space only for a few selections from these letters. Dr. Gunsaulus, of Chicago, says: "The effect on the religious life, in most cases, is very weakening." Dr. Ingersoll, of Brooklyn: "One of the chief hindrances of efficient, consecrated service on the part of young people in Brooklyn is the fascinating enticement of the theater, which, for the most part, bewilder the senses and benumb the conscience." Rev. Smith Baker, now of Minneapolis, after nineteen years of work in Eastern cities, says: "The effect of theater-going was always to deaden their spiritual life and destroy their spiritual influence." Dr. Hawes, of Burlington, Vt.: "As a rule, the-atergoers are not those on whom any pastor can depend when there is a call for special activity, or, indeed, in carrying forward the regular religious work of the church." Dr. Duryea, of Omaha, after speaking of the change of view of many Christians as to the propriety of attending the theater, says: "They fail, as I think, to consider the general influence of the theater as an *institution*, to the discredit of which, it must be said, that it does not keep the stage pure; is willing to pander to the pruriency and lust of the low and sensual, and has no true, deep respect for woman-hood; no chivalric devotion to her purity and honor." Dr. Henry A. Stimson, of St. Louis: "My own conviction is that it is utterly destructive of spiritual life. The theater, if one may judge it by the sign-boards, is just now in the lowest stage of fleshliness and degradation." E. P. Goodwin, D.D., of Chicago, says: "I have half suspected sometimes, when popular plays were being presented, that one might count more church people there than they could at prayer meeting. The effect of theater-going is unquestionably bad. I believe that invariably it chills and hurts all Christian life. If anything may be called *worldly,* saturated through and through with a spirit that antagonizes the Spirit of Christ and his gospel, it is the theater. With us, all theaters, without exception, have Sunday performances; most of them an afternoon matinee as well as an evening entertainment. Furthermore, neither actors nor actresses seem to have any scruples as to traveling and performing on the Sabbath. Liquor saloons flank them on either side, and brothels and gambling dens are known to be within easy reach. After twenty or more years of pretty close observance of their influence, I do not hesitate to say that it seems to me an impossibility to maintain a high Christian standard of either belief or life, and to develop a rounded, rich and potential Christian character, and at the same time to be a habitual or occasional attendant upon theaters. They are of the earth, earthy, and they who are seeking to lead a risen, heavenly life cannot come in contact with them without suffering defilement." Now it is a most remarkable Circumstance that historians, moralists, philosophers and Christians through twenty-seven hundred years should have dreaded and testified against the theater as a moral influence on the race.

II. Let us now look at the theater from another point of view. I hasten to remind you * again that it is not the pure drama that is here under discussion, and that I do not hold that dramatic representation on the boards of the theater is necessarily evil. It may be freely conceded that if it could be separated from all moral taint, conducted by Christian men on Christian principles with a Christian motive, it might be a moral power for good. It has the elements of tremendous influence over the human mind. And Christians, above all others, would rejoice in its exercise if it were safe. But, conceding all this, the *tendency* has been uniformly bad. "Its claim to be a school of morals," says Dr. T. T. Munger, " is false, not because it is immoral, but because it cannot, from its own nature, be a teacher of morals."

What is the matter? The matter is the *motive*. The motive of the theater is money. The managers have absolutely no other. The means are adapted to the end. The scheme is to make a sensation which will draw the crowd, which will bring the *money*. Hence the theater's appeal to the sensibilities and passions is uniformly exaggerated and extreme. Not only do its plots consist of assassinations, poisonings and illicit loves and intrigues, but every passion is overdrawn. "Anger is madness; ambition, frenzy; love, delirium." It does not hold the mirror up to Nature, except in her very worst aspects and her most degraded moods. Nature is not *always* after money. Nature is not always in an agony of either horror or laughter. Nature is not always languishing with a great sorrow on her face and a bottle of laudanum in her pocket, weeping last tears over a false lover. Nature is not always nude, whirling around on one great loe, while the other is up in the air. Nature is not always armed with pistol and bowie knife. Nature is not always roaring through the streets with clenched fists, disheveled hair and blood-shot eye. She is not always cutting throats or playing the harlot. Nature never ridicules religion and morality for an entrance fee. Nature is sane, rational, decently clad, patient, self-contained, not living for cash, even divinely beautiful at times, like her Maker. Now, you can make money, but you cannot teach morals by simply exhibiting treachery and licentiousness. This is the trouble with the theater. Its choice of a theme, its scenic display, its acting a part, all have reference, so far as the management of the institution is concerned, to the ticket office at the door.

Why, then, is the church so uniformly against the theater? Secular papers say it is *religious bigotry*. But the philosophers and historians of Greece and Rome during 600 years, B. C, were not Christian bigots. Plato was no religious crank. The Americans who signed the Declaration of Independence were not bigots. I will not say that there is no religious bigotry about this matter, but the blindest and narrowest bigotry in the case is that *secularism* which will not see that Christians must either keep themselves unspotted from the world, or cease to be Christians. There is no earthly reason why Christians and moralists should oppose the theater, except their dread of its influence as learned from experience; for Christians love a good time as well as other people.

But why not *reform* the theater? That is a legitimate question. Why not? To reform the theater, you must reform four classes—the dramatist, the managers, the actors and the audience—no child's play. Reforms of the theater have been often tried and as often failed. Garrick tried it and failed. Hannah More tried it and failed. Macready tried it and failed. Henry Irving tried it and failed. Edwin Booth tried it and failed. Governments, both ancient and modern, have tried it and failed. New England committees of high minded gentlemen, with every advantage on their side, tried it and failed, sixty years ago. Channing and Lyman Beecher tried it and failed. The hope of that sort of reform is a childish delusion. And yet, without doubt, Christians are bound to bring the gospel to bear upon the theater in some way. The question is, how? The most recent and popular method suggested in these days, is that of *discrimination*. Let the Christian community generally go to the theater whenever a clean, standard drama is put upon the boards, and refuse to go at all other times. This, it is claimed, would encourage the managers to clean out their Augean stables and keep them cleaned. But there are several difficulties with this plan. Its success depends upon whether the managers can get larger incomes from Christian patronage as a whole, than from the world's patronage. Experience and statistics prove that while they bring out a clean play once in twenty times to draw the

Christian public, they can do better financially to cater to the world. The Christian and moral classes of people generally, do not care to go very much even to a pure theater, having, I suppose other and higher concerns on hand; so that the managers cannot afford to depend upon them, and to slough off General Booth's "submerged tenth." And even if Christians were frequent attendants, they would not constitute in New York City more than one-tenth of the numerical patronage which the management would study to please.

There is another difficulty here. The plan does not work in practice. The theater never had a larger per cent, of Christian attendance than today, and it was never more corrupt. This is poor encouragement for this method of reform. The reason is that Christian theatergoers are not there for the purpose of reform, but for enjoyment, or the study of -art. But that is not the worst. The theater is an institution supported by a board of managers, who propose to make money. Now suppose Christians attend on the one clean night (if they have wit enough to find out beforehand which that is) and stay away the twenty dirty nights. What do they support? The *institution*. The same managers receive their support who run the machine the other twenty nights, seven nights in the week. Their money goes into the same till, and pays perhaps in part for the acting of the other twenty nights. Suppose our friend Hans Shellenbarger, who sells liquor in defiance of the law seven days in the week, and is known to be a corrupter of youth, should advertise that one night in twenty he would clear away all signs of liquor and for three hours would sell nothing but Oxford Teachers' Bibles, would you feel it a privilege to go there for your books in order to reform the *saloon?* It is always a serious thing to support even indirectly an immoral institution, but that is not the worst. The influence of the stage on the Christian is as certain as that of the Christian upon the stage, and even more potent, and the tendency is toward a common level. That means death to Christian influence.

What then? Shall we deny ourselves the theater? That would not be a stupendous loss. In the first place the theater is not essential to the enjoyment of dramatic literature. I admit with Vincent, that "the dramatic instinct is natural, but deny that the science accompaniments of the theater are essential to the enjoyment of the dramatic gift." Let great actors become great readers, and the best results may still be secured. Again, the theater is not essential to rational entertainment. Strictly speaking, it is not an amusement which physiologist and moralist can approve. It lacks the essential element of amusement, that is, recreation. Its late hours, scenic allurements, and excessive appeals to the passions make it a dissipation rather than a recreation. A walk, a ride, a pull at the oar, an hour with the bat or football, or an evening with a friend over Hamlet or Macbeth, would be infinitely superior. Still further, the theater is not essential to high intellectual attainments, either in the art of eloquence or music. I know that excellent people go to Paris and Berlin, and forthwith fall in with the theater and opera-going crowd in the interest, they think, of *high art*; but fortunately, high art requires no such low vassalage. Mendelssohn, who was true, we are told, in a lying age, and in an adulterous age, was pure—speaking of a certain lewd operatic performance, said: "Yes all this produces an effect; but I have no music for such things. I consider it ignoble. Therefore, if the present epoch exalts this style, then I will write oratorios." All hail! Mendelssohn!

There are several points in regard to the theater which ought to help Christians and moralists to settle their relations to it: 1. It has a power of fascination for the mind, the tendency of which is to make undue drafts upon attention and to over-stimulate the sensibilities and desires. 2. Its associations are such as to bring one into social contact with the worst elements of society. The theater is a great leveler. The churches and the slums had better be apart. 3. The best theaters of today are breaking down all reverence for the Christian Sabbath, and it is very evident that in that respect they have already contaminated the church. 4. Their method of advertising is a dishonor to our civilization, to say nothing of the Christian church. Only a short time ago the Cleveland Congregational Club, composed of laymen as well as ministers, felt called upon publicly to protest against the vile theatrical posters which were corrupting the children and youth of the city. Not a great while ago, the Cleveland *Plain Dealer* was out with an actually sane sentiment on this subject, urging the ministers to preach against this hideous, corrupting abomination of our time. Even the *Plain Dealer*! 5. The theater, to the frequent attendant, is excessively expensive. Herrick Johnson says: "The receipts of the New York theaters are greater than the expenses of the churches, the schools and the police force combined." 6. It is the testimony of experience and observation through the years, that, explain it as you will, theater-going *deadens the spiritual life.*

Do I advise Christians to totally abstain from the theater? No. Not I. Advice is cheap and seldom followed. I only offer you the facts. For myself I believe in total abstinence. But each individual must decide and his decision must be his own. We are to decide of course, not as worldlings, but as the children of God. Even the Bible does not settle this question for us. It gives us the great principles of the new life, and leaves us to decide in the court of our own souls upon their application. This personal liberty is essential to the building of character. Too much revelation would be just as bad as too little. But we are bound to remember that here lies both the glory and the peril of our probation. Every good man is bound to keep himself in the best possible working trim for the promotion of righteousness. Hence I close with the words of Mazzini to the young men of Italy, in 1848: "Love and reverence the ideal. It is the country of the (spirit—the city of the soul, in which all are brethren who believe in the inviolability of thought and the dignity of immortal natures. Love enthusiasm—the pure dream of the virgin soul, the lofty visions of early youth. Respect above all things your *consciences*. Have upon your lips the truth which God has placed in your hearts. While working in harmony, even with those who differ from you, yet ever bear erect your own banner, and promulgate your own faith."

CHAPTER VI:
THE YOUNG CHRISTIAN
AND THE CARD TABLE

THREE thousand years ago it was said, "Surely in vain the net is spread in the sight of any bird." Yes, "surely," for the bird has such an instinct for self-preservation, that if the net is spread in its sight it will avoid it. But the same can hardly be said of a man. You may spread the net before his very eyes and show him a victim caught and struggling to be free, and yet so great is his confidence in his own power to get out of danger that, sooner or later, he will walk in and make the trial. To catch a bird, you must spread the net in secret; to catch a man you may spread it in open sight. This principle finds ample illustration in the hazards of games of chance.

Let me say, however, to start with, that I do not speak of games of chance as necessarily wrong. What we are chiefly concerned with just now is not the moral nature of a certain act, but the *tendency* of a certain habit. If we speak of card-playing as one of the modern "Beasts of Ephesus," it is not because handling bits of painted pasteboard is essentially a sin, but because the habit is allied with certain associated evils; and this we believe can be made manifest to candid Christian minds. It must be remembered also that the persons now addressed are young Christians who have pledged themselves for life to live and work for the promotion of Christ's kingdom in the earth. Their master passion, therefore, is not simply to do all that statute law allows, or even all that to them is harmless in the line of amusement, but to do that which is expedient for the great cause in which they are embarked.

Granting, then, the abstract sinlessness of a game of cards, the question before us is simply one of *expediency* for a servant and child of God. The policy of the genuine Christian is not simply defensive but aggressive. His supreme end is not to indulge in all that may be escaped from without detriment, but to attain unto all that will render him more efficient in promoting the kingdom of Christ. Every moral act, therefore, whether of work or of play, must be questioned as to the tendency of its influence on the immortal nature, and its immediate influence on our spiritual efficiency as soldiers of Christ. An amusement which is not a recreation but a dissipation, which exhausts vital force and moral stamina instead of recruiting them, should be given a wide berth by Christians. With this understanding, I venture to make the following mild and plain common-sense suggestions:

I. Experience has proved that games of chance have a peculiar fascination for most people, which tends strongly to induce a habit. This fact is based upon the natural craving of the human mind for excitement. That craving is not an evil in itself, but it is to be kept in subjection to reason and conscience. Now there is nothing to be found which so unnaturally feeds and stimulates this craving as the uncertainty and hazards of games of chance. It is probable that the illegal practice and patronizing of lotteries, of which so many Americans have been guilty, are stimulated quite as much by the mere excitement of chance as by the hope of gain. Unquestionably, therefore, almost any game of chance, and especially cards, may be a natural stepping-stone to the sin of gambling. This same principle explains, in part, that modern abomination, the church lottery, which is a species of gambling in the name of religion. This vicious custom is practiced not to eke out the revenue of the State, like that gigantic swindle in Louisiana, but to pay the expenses of the church of Christ! It is done, we are told, with a good motive—done that the gospel may be preached, or that the poor widow and the orphan may be warmed and fed. But is the church to be sustained by blighting its spiritual life? Is the widow's boy to be ruined that the mother may get a ton of coal? Is the public law to be defied and the public conscience debauched in the name of religion? The whole scheme is an agreement with those who say, "Let us do evil that good may come," " whose damnation is just." It is bad enough when Christians fail to sustain the cause of Christ and humanity by sheer neglect, but to turn the very house of God into a den of lottery thieves is yet a lower deep. If, church officers, whether deacons or priests or bishops, when allowing such things should be put in the county jail for setting up a gambling establishment on their premises, as the law directs, it would be a great gain to the cause of righteousness.

2. When the habit of card-playing is once formed, experience proves that it becomes so absorbing that it robs one of time and health and spiritual usefulness. It becomes a passion, a craze. Nights are spent in its indulgence. I know of a certain city church where the prevailing amusement of the members is " progressive euchre," and the testimony of those who know is, that it is killing the spiritual life of the church. It acts as a blight upon the moral health of the young. It dissipates spiritual impres-

sions. It prevents the mind from coming into tender, sympathetic relations to the Savior, and thus defeats the very end for which the church exists. This is not because handling pasteboard is a sin per se, but because the nature of the game unduly engrosses the mind of the child of God as it does that of the unsaved.

3. The *associations* of the card-table are such in spite of all that worldly church members can say, that in the estimation of the world the Christian lowers himself by the use of it. The card-table like the common theater, is a terrible leveler. The reason is that cards are peculiarly, as Dr. Haydn has said, "the tools of the gambler. They are recognized as at home in the dens of vice and shame—in the hands of lewd men and women. It is beyond dispute that cards have ministered far more to vice and dissipation than to sweetness of temper, cleanness of hands and purity of life." To quote the words of another, "The scoundrel in his lair, the scholar in his room, the pirate on his ship, the gay woman at parties, loafers at the street corners, public functionaries in their office, the beggar under the hedge, and some professors of religion in the somnolent hours of the Sabbath, waste their energies in the ruinous excitement of the game." Now it cannot be a mistake for Christians who arc pledged to the service of God to avoid this leveling process.

4. Card-playing leads many to gambling. It arms the temptation to gamble with almost resistless power. I do not confound things sinful with things innocent. In loyalty to truth we are always bound to make distinctions. I believe in innocent amusement. I would conscientiously encourage the innocent that I might condemn the sinful. When, therefore, I condemn social card-playing, it is not on the

same ground on which I condemn gambling. I condemn gambling because it is a sin in itself. I condemn social card-playing because in so large a number of cases *its tendency is to lead to the sin of gambling.* You remember the words of the Lord Jesus: "If thy right hand offend thee, cut it off." Why? It was no sin to have a right hand, and to use it; but if it "*offend* thee, cut it off." "If thy right eye offend thee, pluck it out." Why? It was not wicked to have a right eye and to use it. No, but if it *offend* thee — if it cause thee to sin against thy soul or the soul of a friend — sacrifice it. You remember the words of Paul: "If meat make my brother to offend, I will eat no meat." It was not wrong in itself to eat meat, but if it even innocently led a brother to fall into sin, it was more expensive meat than Paul could afford to eat. There was nothing, not essential to his own spiritual life, that tended even remotely to endanger another soul, which he would not give up. Let us plant ourselves on this Christian principle, and card-tables will disappear from the church of Christ. Let me speak on the matter to young ladies as well as young men. You young ladies are not perhaps absolutely, but you are relatively, stronger, morally, than young men, simply because the snares of the gambler are not laid for you. Being free from this temptation while young men are exposed, are you not thoughtless and cruel with regard to your influence? I have seen boys in school and young men in college and soldiers in camp debauched and ruined by gambling, who, if questioned would say, "I learned to be expert in the handling of cards in the social circle at home, and that prepared the way for my ruin." Have not you, Christian young ladies, seen young men go from the innocent card-table where you sat with them to the gamblers' hell? Had your influence anything to do with their fate? Did you help them to learn that fatal trade? You do not know that you did. But I think you ought, as God's child, *to know that you did not.* The Philadelphia *Ledger* a few years ago, had the following sensible remark:

> "There are so many ways in which girls can be amusing, entertaining and useful to themselves and to others, that it seems a great pity that any of them should resort to the common vices of coarse men. That they do so in the evening entertainments of private and elegant homes, and at the most fashionable summer resorts, appears to be beyond question. And that the results will appear in unlooked-for demoralization in the future of what we call good society may be set down as among the certainties of natural law."

I know that there are conscientious Christian parents who believe in training their children to handle cards at home as a safeguard against the temptation to gamble when away. But the experience of the Christian ages is largely against such a course. It could be easily shown that the boy who remains in total ignorance of the use of cards is far less liable to be drawn into gambling than the boy who has become an expert in the use of them at home. I believe that wise Christian parents will almost instinctively sympathize with Dr. Haydn when he says:

> "For that theory of education which favors training children in the temperate use of wine, the theater, the dance, the card-table and so on—however heroic this treatment may be deemed—we find it impossible to have more respect than for the practice which once prevailed, it is said, among Scythian mothers of

throwing infant children into a running stream of cold water, that only the sturdy—those able to survive the test—might remain on their hands to be reared and educated."

Burdette has said that if you dip your finger into a basin of water and then withdraw it, the hole which is left will be the measure of the influence of good advice upon young men. This may do for a joke, and it may be true with many, but I do not believe it as to the children of God. I know there is a dark side to this subject. History and experience prove that advice is often fruitless. The drunkard and the gambler, in spite of all warnings, examples, facts, philosophies; in spite of the wail of misery that goes up from ten thousand broken hearts and ruined homes from generation to generation, go forward, treading heedlessly above the abysses till they sink into dishonored graves; and their children come marching on in the tracks of their fathers—another long phalanx with doom written upon their banners, to the same dishonored graves. But it is not all dark. I believe in the renewed hearts even of misguided and miseducated young men and young women. They are, they must be, open to the lessons of experience. Standing in the light of God's promise, that his word shall not return unto him void, and that he will help men to be wise for themselves, I speak to all whom it may concern and whose eye may fall upon these words, and call upon all who are tempted to rise and take the true Christian position. The aim of Christ is to break the dominion of all evil over the human mind, to set the soul free, to leave its grand powers untrammeled for the lofty attainments of philanthropy and eternal life. We not only may, but we must, ally ourselves to him, if personal wreck is to be escaped. The cause of morality, the cause of liberty, need—oh, how much they need—the best, the highest, the purest manhood that we can furnish. Humanity, country, the church, our own immortality, all call upon us to take a position now in the service of Christ that we shall not have to repent of when we stand at the judgment bar.

CHAPTER VII:
THE YOUNG CHRISTIAN
AND THE CLUB

I. THE Christian home is the most important spot on this globe. The characteristic difference between civilized and savage life lies in the Christian home. In one of the great crises of human history, when Egypt was shrouded in darkness, so that they "saw not one another, neither rose up any from his place, the children of Israel had *light* in *their* dwellings." The characteristic feature of heathenism is the absence of any true conception of home. They sit near each other in the bonds of heredity, in the terrible power of social influence, but spiritually they do not see each other, "neither can any rise up from his place." Egypt, with all her civilization and all her hoary institution^, had no blessing for humanity. The hope of the race lay simply in those God-lighted homes of Goshen. A great truth was reached when it was made plain that God meant to use the family, the home, as an instrument to build up redeemed society. It is the light of the Christian home to which we must look chiefly for the progress of the race.

A civilized state cannot survive without it. The communism and nihilism which infest our institutions and endanger our national life must find their antidote, if anywhere, in the Christian home. If the multiplication of such homes does not keep pace with the growth of population, society must deteriorate and the state must fall.

II. The Christian church is second in importance

only to the Christian home. The institutions which have become sacred and essential to Americans are the home, the church, the school, and the free government by ballot. These constitute the cordon of defenses which guard the liberty and ennoble the life of the American people. The school-house and the hall of legislation are both the children of the church. The relation which the church sustains to the economics, to the social ethics, to the intellectual life and the spiritual destiny of the nation is such that its removal would remand us to paganism. Anything, therefore, which touches injuriously the home and the church, touches the eye and the soul of the nation, and throws itself across the path of the kingdom of God.

Now it is on this account that I am jealous of clubs. I believe that the vast growth of "club life" in our generation is a menace to both home and church. Let no devotee of clubs, however, imagine that I am going to make an indiscriminate onslaught upon his favorite institution. I believe " a good club is a good thing and a bad one is not." I am well aware that there are all sorts. The bad, however, are very numerous, and are growing more so. There is also an increasing rage for club life generally, which has become epidemic among men and even among some women. The clubs most to be feared are those which are organized chiefly for social purposes, which are confined to men, which become more attractive to husbands and sons than their homes and so compete with home attractions, which are more expensive even for lunching purposes than the best hotels, which cost from one to three hundred dollars for initiation fees, and another hundred, more or less, for annual dues, which are known as drinking places to be quite as dangerous as the saloon, and which are open

Sundays and thus compete with church as well as home attractions. If there are no such places for respectable men, let some one arise and convict me. That the attractions of the club-house are not a myth is pretty clear from the fact that many men belong to a number of clubs at the same time. A "respectable" gentleman, and son of a most worthy Christian man, died in New York not long ago, and although having had a fair income, he left his wife and young family in want. He was at the time of his death a member of ten clubs.

Now many things might be said about such clubs as to their waste of money, their temptation to drink, but my principal point is that the passion for such organizations betrays a dangerous sign of our times, because it threatens both the church and the home. It is certain that Christian young men had better give them a wide berth. If there is any danger threatening American society it is the slight attachment of many men, young and old, to their homes. Few people are aware how society in cities, both here and in England, is honeycombed with clubs, and it would be difficult to find in either country today a thoroughly earnest Christian worker who is not opposed to them. "Usually," says one of our ablest magazines, "the club rooms are open on the Sabbath, often evading the law against Sunday saloons, alluring young men from the services of the church and of the Y. M. C. A. alike. On that one home day, and on all other days, they draw the father and son and brother from the refining fellowship of the home to coarser companionship and conversation."

The pastors of our churches are as a rule awake to the danger of the club. One of them writes me: "Our churches would not be so destitute of men if it were not for the allurements of the club house." Dr. Gunsaulus says, "They most radically interfere with the higher ideals of happiness at home." Dr. Goodwin says, "My opinion about clubs is that they draw men away from their families, offer temptation in the way of card-playing, wine and liquor-drinking, and are among the most subtle and damaging foes of both the home and the church." A New England pastor says, "Clubs are of all sorts, good, bad, indifferent. The best thing that can be said about most of them is that they are not very bad. They are for the most part mere loafing places, *dreary enough* for the man who has a *purpose in life*. Of course they despoil the home. I married a couple recently, and was exhorted to arrive at half-past-six, sharp, as the groom must go to his lodge at seven!" Among others who have expressed positive views on the subject of clubs, one should not forget to read from Thackeray's "Book of Snobs," the chapters on "Club Snobs."

But to speak a little more fully of the home: what is the position which a man occupies in the home, as father, son, and brother? Does he merely furnish the financial basis, and are the mother and sister responsible for everything else that makes the home different from a hotel? Does not the father's time belong to the home out of his business hours just as much as the mother's after the housework is done?

It is not the money furnished by the father's toil, nor the manual labor of housekeeping that *makes the home*. It is the amount of heart put into the home by both father and mother. The man and the woman who do not want a real *heart-home,* have no business to marry. Their interest after marriage is one. Is congenial society what they want? Let them gather such society to themselves in their home. Let there be a revival of the old-fashioned grace of hospitality. The forms and ceremonies of hospitality have almost killed the soul of it. But let us cultivate an independent indifference to the laborious requirements of fashionable society and simply have our friends with us when we choose, without fuss and formality. And " our friends" means not merely those of the father and mother, but of the young folks and children as well. This finding one's society away from home is ruinous to the atmosphere of the home as a center of culture, • which is what it should be. There is no more civilizing influence to children than the having of earnest, Christian, cultivated people as frequent guests. As things are now, the city gentleman too often takes his visiting friend to his club. Now if his friend is a man of worth he inflicts a real loss on his home by not sharing the social pleasure with his dear ones there. All the selfish gratifications, all the luxury, all the congenial company of fellow members of the club will never compensate the father for the losses that will come to his home by means of his absence. His boys are growing daily like their associates. They will not stay at home if he does not. He might in the evening and Sabbath hours be moulding them into the men that he wishes them to be. The simple fact that the father and mother love to be at home, whenever it is possible, is an anchor to the whole family that will hold many a child from drifting out into the current of sin.

Here is what one woman says about it: "It is just as heathenish for a father to withdraw into the luxury of his club when his wife is wearing herself out with the little ones at home, as is the Mormon father's brutal habit of courting a new wife when the woman he first married comes to have her hands tied with the care of children." If the older brother cares to be at home, he will save the younger. Even if the club were all that the best of them claim to be for the individual member, still that member, if he has a family, may have no right to the personal indulgence of membership, if it involves injustice to his wife or neglect of his home. The wife cannot be a good mother if she is a neglected wife, she cannot command the respect of her children, especially her boys. The children cannot be expected to grow up into good men and women if home is not to them "the dearest spot on earth," and it never will be that if slighted by father or mother.

Robert Southey, the poet, in a letter to his friend makes this statement: "I have declined being a member of a literary club which meets at the Chapter Coffee House. Surely a man does not do his duty who leaves his wife to solitude, and I feel duty and happiness to be inseparable. I am happier at home than any society can possibly make me." We may be sure that the home life in that family was refined, sweet and attractive. Now, I do not wish to take any extreme ground as to clubs; but I have hoped, besides warning against the bad, to show the mischief lurking even under the acknowledged advantages of good clubs. And when Christian young men see these dangers to the home and the church; and this tendency to self-indulgent personal habits which is liable to leave neither money nor heart for the Lord's work, I believe they will be the first to deny themselves of what before may have looked like a harmless and even profitable association with their fellows. "If thine eye offend thee, pluck it out. If thine hand offend thee, cut it off." No fanatic uttered these words, but He who came to bring "peace on earth and good will to men," He who is the ideal young man, before the minds of all our young Christians.

To the Christian young man in the city, who has no home, I say: Get one as soon as possible! and in the meantime go to work in church, and Sabbath-school and Y.M.C.A. and you will find companionship and occupation enough, if you are a willing worker.

Chapter VIII:
The Young Christian
and the Dance

IN taking up this subject from the Christian point of view, it is but fair and right that all reasonable concessions should be made, and made at the outset. Whatever positive objections may be urged against the ordinary dance, I for one, am ready to make to the friends of this amusement the following

Concessions:

The dance is not forbidden in the Bible.

It is not necessarily a sin *per se*.

"It is better to dance than to slander our neighbors."

"It is better to dance than to be self-righteous."

Amusements as such are necessary and good. Every human being is entitled to amusement within proper limits.

The dance may sometime tend to cultivate grace of movement.

If conducted for strictly religious purposes, as in the case of David and other cases in the Bible, and when the sex element is eliminated, it will not be harmful.

It may, under certain circumstances, be health-giving.

There may be a certain "rhythm and poetry of motion" in the dance which is pleasing to speculative and ethereal minds, and which has no moral or psychological perils.

If the hearts of young Christians are in the dance more than in the cause of Christ, and if the parents in the home take no stand against it, then all other prohibitions are futile.

Furthermore, I concede that on this general subject there may be good and true Christians whose judgment I respect, though widely differing from my own. The fair thing in every such case is a thorough and candid discussion from both points of view. The importance of the question in its relation to Christian life demands it.

In full view of these concessions, I feel compelled to hold that dancing, as it commonly prevails in society, is a menace to the Christian life and church which needs the immediate, careful and conscientious consideration of all Christian people.

1. And first of all I protest that the only reason for discussing, and the only reason for objecting to the dance, on the part of Christian parents and teachers, springs from their honest solicitude for the welfare of young Christians and the efficiency and spiritual power of the Christian church in the world. On this ground every disciple of Christ is bound to give the subject a reasonable and serious consideration. Why should any man or woman or intelligent church oppose the dance, if it can be shown that it promotes both spiritual and physical good? No sane person does so oppose it. It is the sheerest prejudice and bigotry for any class of people to affirm that Christians are objecting to the dance without experimental reasons, or on merely *a priori* grounds. Why have the old dancing habits of the Christian church been given up in so many places? Why have Christian pastors and parents and organizations in modern times spoken so often and so

strongly against the common dance? Simply because they have found that it was hurtful to the end for which the church exists. All the objections to the dance that I know of are drawn directly from *experience*. The objections may be wrong, but it is right and reasonable that they should be faithfully and conscientiously discussed by all God's people. I protest, once for all, that the Christian religion is not at war with good manners, grace of motion or any safe and innocent amusement.

2. I hold that it is perfectly reasonable to expect a fair and candid consideration of this, as of other questions, by young Christians themselves, unless parents and .teachers fall into the habit of talking to them like cranks; which we do not propose to do. My own experience with intelligent young people is, that they are as reasonable and conscientious on this and kindred subjects as older Christians, when they once *stop and think*. What I plead for here is simply this: "*Think on these things.*" Young people do not object to any calm and sensible queries as to what may injure their physical life and comfort, or their success in business, or their efficiency and power in intellectual pursuits. Why then should there be any sensitiveness about the minutiae of character and spiritual culture, which touch more closely the real man and woman? Why use care and caution as to that which may affect the exterior and the subordinate interests, and take at haphazard that which may " weaken or ruin the more important qualities of the soul?"

3. We confidently believe that if a reasonably just case is fairly made out against the dance, as tending to injure in any degree the purity and power of the Christian life, young Christians will readily refrain. To assume anything

else is to assume that they are not Christians.

Turning, then, to positive views against the dance as generally conducted and participated in by many church members, we have to say:

First, that, as we concede that dancing is not forbidden in the Bible, neither is it commanded. Christ did not dance, that we know of, and left no command that his disciples should. But all that this proves either way is that the purpose of the Scriptures is to give general principles for the new life, and so leave us the great benefit of deciding for ourselves, in view of those principles and in the light of personal experience, how we shall apply them in a given case. There can be no doubt that this is a part of divine wisdom. It is essential to the building of righteous character that we all should be permitted, nay required, to decide cases of casuistry which affect spiritual life, each one for himself in the court of his own soul, and in the sanctuary of his closet, where he communes with God.

Secondly, we wish to say the dance is not a necessity to amusement and recreation. Every individual is entitled to amusement and recreation. The demand for it is itself the gift of God. But the dance does not constitute any essential part of it. If, therefore, there is any serious objection to the dance on moral or other grounds, we are under no necessity whatever to rescue or reclaim it from its attendant perils. We can all, if we choose, have all the amusement and recreation which our natures require or can wisely bear, without resorting to anything the inevitable tendency of which is to abuse and danger.

Thirdly. Experience has demonstrated, as I shall show further on, that devotion to the popular dance, even in its best and most conservative form, is not only not fitted to promote the highest elements of character, but on the other hand that it makes people less open and sensitive to religious truth. The Rev. Dr. H. M. Tenney, who was for several years the wise, and cautious, and efficient pastor of a city church where dancing prevailed, says: "I have found that those under the spell of these amusements (dancing, card playing, etc.) are the hardest to reach with the truth. They are the last to be reached and the first to backslide. If others have had a different experience, I have yet to hear of it." If it be said that it is not in the use but only in the abuse of the dance, that the evil lies, and that any and every good thing when abused becomes an evil, then we are compelled to take issue on that point. The evil tendency lies not in the abuse, but in the nature of the thing. Out of all the multitudinous forms of amusement there is hardly one in fifty that is, from its nature, at all liable to serious moral abuse. The promiscuous dance from its very nature, like card playing and wine drinking, is extremely liable to such abuse. Not that it is often engaged in with evil motives; not that it cannot be practiced without evil thoughts; but no one will deny that there is in the dance where both sexes are mingled an undue excitement, a peculiar and absorbing fascination, an extreme tendency to excess and dissipation, which is found in connection with almost no other, amusement, and which high spiritual life seldom withstands. Dr. Jas. H. Jackson, of Dansville, N. Y., while believing in the physical benefit of the dance if it can be kept within certain safe limits, makes the following state-ment: "As dancing is generally conducted by those who take part in it, I have no hesitation in saying that the evil far overbalances the good that comes from it; so that it is indefensible, and should not be sustained by Christians."

After speaking of the physiological dangers of the dance, he refers to its dissipating effects upon the mind; and specifies dissipation, mental perversity, loose habits of thought, weakened conscience, unfitness for public duty, destroyed sense of allegiance to God, " and thus the person is prepared to be influenced wrongly in a social way."

Fourthly. This brings us to the real core of the Christian objection to the dance—it is naturally dangerous to social purity. Its chief fascination lies in the relation of the sexes. Take the element of sex out of the problem and the dance need not be feared. But as it is generally conducted it brings the sexes into improper relations to each other, and thus sets the passions on fire. It is useless to mince matters on this point. The danger of the promiscuous dance lies in the too familiar handling of each other's persons when the sexes are together. When we add to this the dissipating and fascinating attendant circumstances, and especially the modes of female dress usually adopted for the dance, affording exposure of arms and neck and bosom, it is impossible to doubt the existence of moral peril. The form of dress is doubtless innocently adopted, but it is nevertheless a vulgar and subtle, though unintentional, temptation to young men of both pure and impure mind. Christian young men who have previously been habitual dancers have repeatedly made this confession. Said one, when asked wherein lay its fascination: "To speak frankly, it lies in personal contact." Said a Philadelphia army officer when first witnessing a round dance: "If I should see a man offering to dance with my wife in that way, I would horsewhip him." We do not at all mean to imply that many ever join in such a dance with deliberate evil intent, but only that it blunts certain natural instincts of modesty and propriety which were intended of God for the guarding of virtue, by allowing daring familiarities which would not be tolerated anywhere else. No wonder that such a large and liberal minded man as Horace Bushnell should say of these forms of the dance: "They are the contrived possibilities of license which belong to high life only when it runs low." No wonder Gail Hamilton says with her usual force: "The very pose of the parties suggests impurity." The chief of police has said that "Three-fourths of the abandoned girls of New York were ruined by dancing." Even the *Police Gazette* once said: "Strange that young ladies will allow gentlemen to assume positions and take liberties in the public dance that they would not allow in their parlors."

It has been said by still another, " The dancing hall is the nursery of the divorce court and the training ship of prostitution."

Now, I do not endorse all this strong language, but I quote these sentences because candid and thoughtful people know that there is at least a terrible basis of truth for such views. Allow me to make at this point two other quotations from earnest and well-balanced men. A young city pastor writes me: "When I came to make up my mind for myself as to my own personal practice and my advice to others, I decided that the way in which I had been brought up (and in which I continued while dependent upon my parents, out of regard for their wishes and feelings, if for no other reason), was on the whole the best way. I decided this before I became a minister, and the more I have traveled and the more I have seen of life in the country and in city, the stronger has been my conviction that total abstinence from dancing, theater-going and card-playing, is the wisest, safest and happiest course." Prof. Amos R. Wells says: "Dancing like all Gaul—is divided into three parts: One third is esthetic, one-third is physical exercise, one-third is sensual. As to the first—-the enjoyment of the fine music, of beautiful dresses, of forms and motions—these may all be had under better auspices than in the dance. A woodland ramble, a tennis tournament, an archery club, bicycle or horseback riding, the concert-room: these furnish in God's own way tenfold more beauty to the eye and ear than is furnished by the finest ball ever given. As for the second third, the physical exercise, it is ill-timed, ill-placed, ill-environed. Hot air, gaslight, excitement, midnight crowds, loaded supper tables, noise: these make a poor outfit for a gymnasium. Every honest investigator of the dance as now practiced in America, will agree that the third part into which this heathen Gaul is divided is the stronghold of the province. The sensuality of the dance makes bold-eyed women of soft-eyed maidens; it makes swaggering rakes of pure lads; it changes love to flirtation and a game of flippant shrewdness; it makes applicable to manly America Tolstoy's terrific strictures on ignoble Russia. It never recreates a Christian; it *discreates* a Christian and creates a sensualist." It cannot be denied that the dance, even in its best form, almost universally leads to excess; that it declines to keep within the limits of recreation and runs to dissipation; that it often tends to create jealousy between the husband and wife; that like the theater it is practically impossible to reform or reclaim it from abuse; that "the square dance cannot be kept square, but is sure to be rounded off with the waltz," that "as practiced by the world it has about the same relation to immorality that wine sipping has to drunkenness," that "abstinence, therefore, is much more easily practiced than temperance;" and that they who speculate on its being divorced from danger and made a perfectly and spiritually healthful exercise, probably do not understand human nature and are only wasting their time.

Fifthly. Now as to the effect of this habit of dancing on the life of the Christian church, when practiced by church members, there is a remarkable unanimity of testimony which earnest-minded young Christians surely cannot afford to overlook. It is a very rare thing to find a devoted and efficient Christian worker who is a dancer. I can learn of no man or woman with a decidedly evangelistic spirit who approves of the dance. It is equally difficult to find any church members who are regularly and helpfully at the prayer meeting who are at all given to the dance. I have not been able to discover any church which is known far and wide as a power for the kingdom of Christ whose members to any large extent patronize the dance. My own uniform experience during more than twenty years of work has been that fathers and mothers who were most earnestly devoted to the moral well-being of their children, and to the progress of the kingdom of God, have shunned and dreaded the influence of the dance. I know of noble Christian parents who removed their family from a certain city, simply to escape that influence. I have corresponded with nearly a hundred prominent pastors and laymen in different parts of the country on this subject, and a very large proportion of the replies are squarely against the practice of dancing by church members, while only five, in a very guarded and qualified way, approve. A few think there are other things just as injurious, which is undoubtedly true. We all know the position taken by such men as Moody and B. Fay Mills on this question.

Now in saying these things chiefly to young Christians, some of whom may be in the habit of promiscuous dancing, I am specially anxious to avoid exerting any hasty, crude, or undue influence in this matter. My one desire is, that my readers should stop and think, and decide the matter for themselves. That seems to be but fair. I am well aware that no church rules or *ex cathedra* prohibitions are of any use, unless the heart and judgment of Christians go with them. If the experience of mature Christian workers, the world's need of consecrated lives, the obligations of our church covenants, and the testimonies I have tried hereto present, when duly and candidly considered, do not convince Christian minds; then, there is nothing for it but "On with the dance." On the other hand, if these considerations should convince any dancing reader that he had better not, then I beseech you, don't sit down and mourn over the loss of your favorite amusement and give it up simply because conscience says you must; but give it up cheerfully and joyfully for the sake of your Lord and Redeemer, and to make room for a larger life and a nobler joy.

O ye highly honored and richly endowed young disciples, called with a high calling to bear the great name and walk in the luminous steps of the Son of God! Do not dishonor that calling. Do not be afraid to exchange the pleasures of the flesh for the joys of the Spirit. If the dance or any other amusement is a hindrance to your Christlike efficiency, cast it from you for His dear sake. Look at the poor world through His eyes. Behold its needs, its sufferings, its blindness, its tears and its guilt; hear its inarticulate cry for spiritual help, and put yourselves eagerly under His supernal banner to answer that cry.

In conclusion, I simply make two quotations which I respectfully ask thoughtful mothers to ponder; throwing in this parenthesis, that while youth are in the home and dependent upon .their parents, the parents' judgment should in all cases settle such a question as this, and no attempt should be made on the part of the young people to override that judgment. The late Dr. Howard Crosby, so forward in matters of reform in New York, makes this statement:

"The foundation for the vast amount of domestic misery and domestic crime which startles us often in its public outcroppings was laid when parents allowed the sacredness of their daughters' persons and the purity of their maiden instincts to be rudely shocked in the waltz. This vice, by the force of fashion and 'good society,' has captivated the young and deluded the old in the church of Christ, and no minister of Christ must utter an uncertain sound here."

Bishop Coxe of western New York says:

"The gross, debasing waltz would not be tolerated another year if Christian mothers in our communion would only set their faces against it and remove their daughters from its contaminations and their sons from that contempt of womanhood and womanly modesty which it begets."

CHAPTER IX:
THE YOUNG CHRISTIAN'S NIGHTS AND SUNDAYS

NO intelligent person will doubt that nights and Sundays are among the most wise and beneficent arrangements of God for our good. The night for physical and intellectual recuperation of exhausted powers; the Sunday for the same, but also more especially for the keeping of the sense of God in the world and the culture of our higher spiritual nature. To pervert these to any other uses than those which God intended is a blow at our own good and the good of society. A certain writer has said that "the great difference between young men, with regard to the work of self-improvement, comes from the different manner in which they employ their leisure time. How are your evenings spent? To what employment is your Sunday generally devoted? Answer that question and I will tell you with almost absolute certainty whether you are growing better or worse in character. If I am to decide on a man's character, I desire to know nothing more than this: How are his evenings and his Sundays passed?"

This intimates that leisure hours rather than work hours are the time to wisely estimate the difference, not only between good and bad men but between good and bad tendencies. We all know that parents, employers, college officers cannot safely judge a boy's character by his conduct while the task is on. They have to wait and see what he does with his nights and Sundays. It is then that temptations come and men fall, if they fall at all. "They that sleep," said the apostle, "sleep in the night, and they that are drunken are drunken in the night." Every foul deed, every bad passion, seeks the darkness and requires leisure. Thousands of men, young and old, will work hard all day and appear outwardly as well as the best, as long as the day's work lasts; but when night comes they are off into dissipation and self ruin.

It is probably manifest to all that these seasons of cessation from toil and care, which we all covet, and which were clearly designed of God to be our safeguard against evil, are really turned by many into the seasons of the greatest danger. Christian people whose aim is to make the most of themselves, seize these hours with grateful eagerness to improve their minds and fortify their spiritual life. The men on the moral down-grade seize the same hours to gratify appetite and passion.

There can be no doubt that among immoral people, Sunday witnesses more sin than any other day in the week. The grievous thing about it is that our Heavenly Father designed Sunday to have exactly the opposite effect. He designed it to be a day not only of rest for the weary, but a day of rational good cheer, a day of high opportunity, a day for the counteracting of the depressing effects of care and toil, and for the fortifying of all that is good and true. When rightly used it becomes the most beneficently educating influence we have. No other earthly boon conferred on society can be compared with it. Dr. John Lord, after all his study of history, ancient and modern, says, "To the Sabbath, and to public preaching, Christendom owes more than to all other sources of moral elevation combined."

Now when these supreme gifts are perverted, of course

there comes a reaction. The very times which God meant to be used to mitigate our hardships and make the soul safe become the season when many men are most defenseless. We read that when Ptolemy laid siege to Jerusalem, the city was well-nigh impregnable by nature; but the Jews foolishly believed that they must not even defend themselves on the Sabbath. Ptolemy soon learned that fact and of course made his assault on that day, and the city, being undefended, was taken. So it is with souls. Satan captures multitudes on Sunday, because, although on that day above all others they ought to be and might be most secure, yet, having perverted the day from God's gracious purpose, they are then most defenseless. Thus we have a new illustration of the fact that the best gifts of God, when perverted, are attended with the most disastrous results.

Now I mention these things to put every Christian reader on his guard against the thoughtless perversion of leisure time. As to evenings, I will only say this in passing: As you value your eternal life, as you hope to honor Christ, try to have a good purpose, a good companion and a good book on hand when the day's work is done. Do not leave your leisure time open to the solicitations of the devil. While you have a home avoid the street and be true to the family circle. Cultivate a Christian conscience, and do not forget that " Conscience belongs to your leisure no less than to your working time."

On the use of Sunday, I beg leave to make two or three further suggestions. I appeal now, as always when touching this theme, to the disciples of Jesus Christ. For I have no hope that those who habitually ignore God, break his laws in other matters, will take to heart the question of the Sabbath. The hope of Sabbath reform is with the Christian church. We have a right to expect, and do expect, a high and commanding position on this subject on the part of those who love the Lord Jesus.

We do not ask any Christian to take extreme ground. What Christian people are contending for is not what is sneeringly called the "Puritan Sabbath." That which is asked for is simply the Christian Sabbath, that large-minded conception of the value of the Lord's Day in its relation to ourselves, the nation and the kingdom of Christ, which Christianity endorses. Public sentiment is swinging now with fearful momentum from the Christian to the Parisian Sabbath. I ask you, young Christians, who are strong and hopeful, to brace yourself against this immoral drift.

First, because it is essential to your own spiritual life. Unless the spirit of simplicity, purity, self-control prevails we cannot live a Christian life at all. Lose the spirit of self-denial and the noble, heroic austerity, if you choose to call it so, the consciousness of having a high calling and a great mission, and you not only will be, but you are already, cut loose from Christ. This Sabbath observance for Christians is not simply a question of following a given rule, or keeping one day in seven in a given way; it is the question of taking up our cross and following Christ. It is not merely our usefulness as children of God, but our spiritual life that is at stake.

Moreover, it is not simply a question of what is most easy and convenient for us now, but what habits of life shall we form, and how do we propose to educate the future. Who does not know that spiritual declension in the church begins in a vast majority of cases by some perversion or abuse of the Sabbath? Every Christian is standing today in the presence of a fearfully low public sentiment on this subject. Resistance to it must and does begin when Christian life begins, and must and does continue as long as Christian life continues.

For example, it is certain as the sunlight, that the printing and selling of a low-toned secular newspaper on the Sabbath, not as a necessity, not as a philanthropic affair, but simply as a business enterprise for the money there is in it, as we all know it to be, and the patronizing of such a paper by Christians, is indirectly a blow at everything which Christianity proposes to propagate among men. I know not how all church covenants read, but there is probably hardly an evangelical church covenant in the country that is not indirectly violated whenever Christians patronize the Sunday paper. It prepares the way for every other business enterprise to claim Christian patronage on the Sabbath, and thus the utter secularization of the Lord's Day is ushered in. It is high time that Christians were done letting Sunday newspaper men bulldoze them into silence and acquiescence. To be sure it is said, "If you fight this thing you will split the church." The statement is not true. The only split will be between the church and the world. Christ came to lay the ax at the root of the tree, not the branches. He came with his fan in his hand. He came for the " baptism of the Holy Ghost and of fire," and ever since, the men who really follow him have had to turn the world upside down, for it is naturally wrong side up.

To be sure we are told the Sunday paper and Sunday postal work and trains and the Sunday saloon "have come to stay." Of course they have if they can. But to the disciple of Christ nothing has certainly come to stay but the kingdom of God. "Come to stay" is begging the question. Suppose a burglar comes into your home, takes your money, eats your food, insults your family, and after kindling a comfortable fire, sits down and announces, "I've come to stay." If you are a man, much more if you are a Christian, you will gird up your loins and roll up your sleeves and say, " We will now proceed to settle that question."

The second reason for bracing ourselves against this secularizing drift is the patriotic one. If we believe in a Christian civilization for our country, the Sabbath must be kept as a religious institution. The following propositions I hold to be absolutely true; (1) You cannot have a Christian civilization with Christ and his precepts left out. (2) You cannot have Christ in our civilization without the Christian church. (3) You cannot maintain the Christian church without the Christian Sunday. There is precisely the same reason for maintaining the Christian observance of the Sabbath on patriotic grounds that there is for the preaching of the gospel itself. Few people will doubt that high morality and pure patriotism are inseparable; and the lesson of history is that morality and Sabbath-keeping also go hand in hand. Society is degraded as Christianity is corrupted, and Christianity is corrupted as the Sabbath is perverted. Mere financial prosperity cannot make men great except "in craft and politics and business calculation." Mere material greatness and numbers cannot create a high moral sentiment, or build a great college, or exalt a state unless there is moral vitality and lofty self-restraint in citizen, teacher and student alike. Only when men are "uncorrupted by the vices of self-indulgence and unseduced by the pleasures of a factitious life" can they do anything to help the nation. Voltaire said, "You cannot kill Christianity as long as the Sabbath is maintained as a sacred day." Why? Because the Sabbath is the day when the gospel of Christ gets at the people. He was shrewd enough to see where the strength of Christianity lay, while many Christians of our day do not seem to discover it.

Hence we say again, self-sacrifice cannot survive without religion, and religion and our country are bound up forever with the observance of the Christian Sabbath. It is on this ground that every Christian and every patriot ought to fight to the last, for the Sunday closing of the Columbian Exposition. I believe that in the last analysis we must hold not only the commissioners but also the government of the United States itself responsible, if that great national business enterprise is open on the Lord's Day. If the government has appointed men to take charge of so momentous a national enterprise as the Columbian Exposition, who have no just appreciation of the moral integrity and honor of the nation, then the settling of the Sunday question ought not to be left to such commissioners. The responsibility is with the appointing power.

These considerations of the relations of national morality to the observance of the Sabbath may be laughed at by the saloon-keeper and the Sunday publisher who propose to make money at the expense of public morals, but surely no Christian can afford to laugh.

My space permits me to offer but one remark more. It is of extreme importance that they who are preaching, or who are going to preach the gospel, should be roused to right convictions on this subject. God forbid that I should misjudge my brethren in this or any other matter; but the evidence seems to be that the majority of pastors have been negligent of duty in trying to enforce the Word of God upon the minds of old and young in its bearing on the Sabbath question. We hear of comparatively very few preaching on this theme, and there is no subject on which it is more difficult to get up an enthusiastic convention than this. Frequently in such a convention the most able and popular speakers have the merest ghost of an audience. If the pastors were awake and active, surely the people could not be so apathetic. That the same trouble seems to prevail in Great Britain is indicated by the fact that a prize of fifty pounds has recently been offered in Scotland for the best essay on "A Christian minister's duty with reference to the Sabbath." The author who took the prize, says: "Let the ministers of our land have the full light of the Bible concerning God's mind on the Sabbath, and their own duty in relation to it streaming into their minds, and the problem is solved. If from the central position which the ministers occupy, laxness on their parts leads to indifference in others, it is just as true that luminous and full-orbed conviction on their part will tell powerfully in the same direction."

CHAPTER X:
THE YOUNG CHRISTIAN
AND THE SABBATH

IN THE preceding number, we have spoken of the young Christian's use of the Sabbath from the point of view of leisure time. But the subject would be quite inadequately discussed without some consideration of the profounder topic of the attitude of the churches into which young Christians are united, toward Sabbath desecration. The question is, to what extent are Christian people responsible for public sentiment in regard to Sabbath observance? The settling of this question, that is, the position now taken by the churches into which young Christians are born, will do much to determine the Christian life of the next generation.

Probably all Christian people will assent to the following propositions:

1. The Sabbath is made for man. It is an institution given of God. It is a boon and not a burden.

2. The maintenance of the Sabbath is essential to the success of the gospel, and hence to the well-being of the race.

3. There is just now in our country an amazing disregard and desecration of the Sabbath.

4. The Christian church itself has very largely fallen into this sin of Sabbath desecration.

5. The remedy for the evil lies primarily with the church.

6. If the church cannot save the Sabbath, it can neither save itself nor the world.

With these propositions in view, let us look first at the cause of Sabbath desecration. We are sometimes told that the cause of Sabbath desecration in our day is a reaction from the overstrict Sunday laws of colonial times. I do not think that is true. Not one in ten thousand knows anything about the colonial Sabbath laws, or ever thought of associating his present practice with the Puritan Sabbath as a cause. Nor is the cause want of proper legislation. The Sunday laws of the country are vastly in advance of the practice of the people. The whole system of Sabbath desecration has grown up not from lack of law, but in defiance of law. Every State in the Union, except California and Arizona, has Sunday laws prohibiting ordinary labor and traffic, except those of "necessity and mercy." The cause is not the change from the seventh to the first day of the week. There never was a more superficial blunder than to maintain that the reason people desecrate the Christian Sabbath is because we are trying to keep the wrong day. The real cause has many phases. I will specify but three:

1. The tremendous and universal spirit of self-indulgence, the love of luxury and pleasure, and the love of money for pleasure's sake.

2. Foreign immigration. These millions of immigrants, 800,000 a year, do not come here as our fathers did, for liberty of conscience, but for bread. They come from the lands of the lost Sabbaths, and without either knowledge of or respect for our American Lord's Day. They are not to blame for this, but we are, for not enlightening them. "It is not health, but disease that is contagious."

3. The saloon. The liquor business is the school where

lawlessness and godlessness are cultivated on principle, and where Sabbath desecration is a part of the stock in trade. The worst result of this "scourge of God," which openly defies all Sunday laws, is its tremendous influence on public sentiment with reference to laws in general. When the honest grocer or dry goods merchant sees the saloon-keeper with open shop on Sunday, setting the law at defiance, of course he asks: "Why should not I have the same privilege? If he is allowed to sell that which debauches society, why "should I heed a law which prevents me from supplying men's legitimate demands?" And so he opens his store; and the law is a dead letter. This discriminating toleration in favor of drunkard makers and corrupters of youth is more than many characters can bear. The sight of grog-shops scooping in the earning of working men on the Sabbath for that which only curses them, leads many a citizen to open his store and get a part of the trade. His conscience gives way to his mercantile ambition; then the value of his testimony against lawbreaking is lost. The same is true of other departments of traffic. The godless merchant not only claims the right to travel in the interest of his business on Sunday, but also to have his goods transported. The Christian merchant under the pressure of competition feels that he must do the same or fail. Hence the gross injustice to the railroad men, and the general defiance of Sunday law. So also godless publishers press their Sunday papers on the community, and Christian people living in a low spiritual atmosphere, satisfy their secular curiosity on Sunday morning by reading them. Thus the church and the world are constantly acting and reacting on each other, and tending to find a common level. The church of God first acquiesces, then patronizes, then defends, until its power to help the world is gone.

The great want, then, is not better laws, but better public sentiment. Not more law, but more conscience.

The most discouraging phase of the Sunday question is the decay of reverence for law in general. Look at it. The old colonial Sunday laws were some of them grotesque and unreasonable. But notice, these rigid laws were not a dead letter. John Barnes was fined thirty shillings for Sabbath breaking. For a second offence "he was set in the stocks and whipped at the post." It is not the wisdom of these laws we commend, but the law-abiding spirit. I say these rigid laws were enforced. The magistrate was on the side of the law, and the people at the back of the magistrate. How is it now? Our Sunday laws are mild and reasonable in the extreme, but they are a dead letter. What does this mean? It means a decay of reverence for law. It means the sup planting of the great idea of duty by the exaggerated notion of liberty and license. Now, I say, this is the most discouraging phase of the Sunday problem. Mr. Evarts truly said: "The welfare of the country depends not on the laws in the book, but on the laws that are enforced."

Another phase of the subject is the too common acquiescence of Christian people in this state of things. Of course, but few Christians openly approve Sabbath desecration; but many say, the Sunday paper has come to stay, the railroad traffic will go on, the Sunday mails must be carried, the saloon cannot be closed, cheese factories will run on Sunday, " the people are set on mischief;" and so we might as well read the Sunday secular paper when it is printed, we might as well send our milk to the factory since it is open anyway, we might as well take the Sunday train to attend to our secular business since the train is running whether we go or not. Yes, and we might as well license the saloon, for it will be open seven days in the week in any case. What is the use of Christian people incurring the odium of the world by struggling against the inevitable? Let us rather adapt ourselves to the circumstances and do as well as we can. That is the way we begin to talk.

It reminds one of the case of Aaron when he had made the golden calf. What an imbecile defense he offered when the prophet of God came down from the mountain. Instead of standing as a man in his high position ought to have stood, making public sentiment, he simply succumbed to the low public sentiment of the hour and laid the blame on " the people": "I am not to blame, the people are set on mischief. I just took their jewels and put them into the fire, and there came out this calf." It is to be feared that many a Christian church is repeating that argument today. Whenever the church adapts itself to the public sentiment of the world, it is doomed. It ought to make Christians blush to know that some of the strongest words against the desecration of the Sabbath by railroad traffic have been uttered by railroad men. The timidity of Christians springs from the assumption that railroad traffic, which keeps 250,000 men at work on Sunday, is a "necessity." But many railroad managers deny the fact. If any railroad business is justifiable on the Sabbath, it is that which has to do with perishable freight; but Robert Harris, of the Union Pacific road, says even freight business is not a necessity on Sunday. Freight business was not carried on on Sunday until the time of the war, and we did well enough without it. He says: "The business men in the cities have no right to demand that their fellow men on the railroad shall work for them on Sunday to bring their goods to hand while they enjoy their liberty." Samuel Sloan, of the Delaware, Lackawana & Western Railway, says: "The necessity for Sunday trains does not exist." The president of a Wisconsin Railway says: "It is practicable to abolish Sunday work." Col. Wright, of the Massachusetts Bureau of Statistics, says: "The way to diminish Sunday trains is to diminish the patrons of them." Gen. A. S. Diven, a man of vast experience, submits the following propositions:

1. Traffic will be substantially the same per week whether moved in 168 hours or 144 hours.
2. It can be moved in 144 hours.
3. The extra cost will be compensated by improved service.
4. There is no public necessity requiring Sunday service.

I apply these propositions to all service in time of peace, both passenger and freight.

If this be true of freight business, it must be emphatically so of all other branches of Sunday labor. No one can honestly maintain that a Sunday paper, or cheese factory, or open store, or saloon is either a necessity or a mercy. They are simply a selfish convenience.

Why then this timidity and discouragement on the part of Christian people in grappling with this tremendous hindrance to the kingdom of Christ?

Christians are surely responsible for the desecration of the Sabbath to the extent of their ability to prevent it. In 1886 there was one communicant to 4.8 of the population of the United States; one evangelical church to 518 souls; one minister to 692 souls. Who can estimate the power of such a body to prevent Sabbath desecration, if only united and loyal to the gospel of Christ? We must assume that church members are either real Christians, or are subject to church discipline. Real Christians are willing to forego even some legitimate luxuries for the sake of promoting the kingdom of God, much more the vices which are sapping the foundations of spiritual life, destroying all reverence for law. There is just as much reason for encouragement in urging this as any other form of gospel truth. We have had some marked encouragement even in Ohio, notwithstanding the liquor oligarchy and the cowardly utterances of some partisan political papers of the State.

It seems to me perfectly clear, therefore,that what the Sabbath reform requires is not primarily more legislation, not an attack on railway companies or publishing companies, but an awakening of Christian principles, an arousing of Christian conscience and devotion on the part of the people at large and especially in the bosom of the church. What have we to oppose to the rapacity of commercial and industrial competition, or to the insolent dictation of law-defying liquor men? Nothing, I believe, but the church of Jesus Christ; nothing but the law of God. If that falters, all hope is gone. It is not the province of the church directly to make Sunday laws, but it is its province to make the sentiment which makes the laws and sustains them. Christ did not commit his cause to the civil magistrate or to the law makers of the Roman Empire. He said to his disciples, "Ye are the salt of the earth."

The first responsibility resting upon the church is to help sustain the Sunday laws of the state. They are far in advance of the sentiments of many professing Christians.

But the church is also bound to help the world "remember the Sabbath day to keep it holy." Its mission is not simply conservative, but aggressive. It is the one institution which is to stand when thrones and tyrannies are passed away. It never stands simply for what is, but always for what ought to be. The true church is not, as the Socialists tell us, in favor of the present order of things. It is an eternal agitator. It never acquiesces in the conditions of the present as long as there is a wronged or suffering soul. Politicians, parties, institutions may work simply to conserve what is, but the church of God has a different mission. No custom of society, however venerable, no prestige of class or position, no alarm about personal liberty, falsely so-called, no laws of states however powerful, can ever nullify that eternal "ought to be" toward which the Christian church must urge its prayer and perpetually press its aim. If it fails of this, there is nothing to take its place.

The laws are a dead letter because moral sentiment is low, and because a mercenary spirit of acquiescence, which is sapping the foundations on which all laws are based, has crept even into the church. As a Cincinnati pastor said two years ago, the church is faithful enough in presenting the sentimental, the esthetic, the tender side of religion, but too lax in pressing the manly, vigorous, aggressive side of the gospel.

How, then, is the church to become the power which its divine mission warrants and which the cause demands?

In general, it is plain that to accomplish anything in this cause, the church must clear its own skirts. "Be ye clean that bear the vessels of the Lord." It must apply the principle, "Physician, heal thyself." This surely is fundamental. It is an inconsistency at which the world will justly laugh, for Christians to complain of railroad companies, while they patronize the Sunday trains; or demand that their goods shall be carried on Sunday, while they piously attend church. It is an inconsistency for churches to condemn the publishers of Sunday secular papers, while hundreds of their members spend Sabbath morning reading them.

And so with all other forms of Sunday desecration. It all comes to this: that churches must stand by their principles or else hold their peace. Their weakness in all moral reforms is their partial complicity with the wrong. I am only claiming that church members should be honest enough to stand by their profession. We are making the future. And if this deteriorating process goes on, it need not be a matter of surprise to anyone to see laws become less and less a barrier to wrong, and religion less and less a power to lift the world. Fathers and mothers of this generation need not be surprised if their children seem to stand on a lower spiritual plane, and have greater obstacles to moral manhood and womanhood" to overcome than they themselves had. And the children of this generation need not be astonished at the brood of evils that shall come in upon them in later years. For their own fathers and mothers, many of them in the church of Christ, have helped to open the door by which the evils are coming in. This apathy of the church, this self-indulgent spirit -of the present age, with respect to this subject, is a piece of infinite cruelty to the next generation of Christians. Let the Christian church purify itself. That is the essential condition of all right influence.

To accomplish this, the first step is to agitate; agitate kindly, lovingly, but firmly, not with passion, but with argument and the Word of God. Keep the subject hot and pressed upon the public mind, till the church shall feel its duty. Christian agitation in this, as in other reforms, is

God's weapon, which the church is bound to wield.

Second. Press the Word of God. It is well enough to urge on physical grounds the importance of the law which secures one day of rest from toil in every seven; but after all, it is this Word of God that sustains the sentiment which sustains the law. If there is no great moral principle behind the Sunday law it cannot stand. If the sense of God and eternity is not kept in the world, no law of mere physical expediency will long remain. The selfishness of one-half of the world will compel the other half to work seven days in the week. The final bulwark of the Sabbath is not the social, or the legal, but the religious sentiment. The business of the church is to propagate that sentiment and to keep the sense of God in the world. So, I say, we must press the Bible. We must stand, like our fathers, by " the Book, the Day, and the Church." The Sabbath must be made to appear as it is, as sustaining a definite relation, not simply to men's physical comfort, but to men's eternal weal, and as involving an eternal obligation to God — or the whole matter will sink to the level of mere humanitarian expediency, which men will accept or reject according as it suits their selfish ends.

Third. If the church is to have any manly force on this subject, it must make it a condition of membership that communicants shall "remember the Sabbath day to keep it holy." It must be understood that the habitual patronizing of any of these Sabbath-breaking institutions on the Sabbath, shall be a disciplinable offense. In many places this cannot be done at once. Agitation and Christian discussion must precede, but it can be done. We need not fear to take high ground on this subject. The laws of God and the laws of the state, together with the prayers of overtaxed millions, are at our backs. Before a united and determined and consecrated church no evil can stand.

The immediate danger is silence and inaction. I know there are difficulties in the way of this reform, and these difficulties multiply more and more as we lower our standard and lose the spirit of Christ. But they can be and must be overcome if the kingdom of God is to prevail.

My appeal, then, is to the men and women of God. I ask you to consider what the Christian Sabbath has been to you and yours. Think of the inseparable connection between it and your Christian life. Think of the blessed calm it has brought to you in the midst of corroding cares, the respite it has given you from crushing toil, the aspirations it has awakened for a better life. Think how essential it is to the progress of Christ's kingdom. Think of the vows you have taken to sustain God's cause, and the mighty obligations you are under to meet the moral needs of the world. And then see if you can afford, for any paltry convenience, to lower the public reverence for law, or to sacrifice the priceless treasure of the Sabbath.

I appeal to my brethren in the ministry, with whom the immediate responsibility rests, to discuss the subject frequently, broadly, fearlessly, in the spirit of the Master, till Christ's principles are enthroned in the hearts of the rich and poor.

Chapter XI:
The Young Christian
and Social Purity

DO I run some risk in touching publicly this theme? Be it so. The importance of the subject will justify the risk. Polite licentiousness is one of the greatest hindrances to the kingdom of God today as it was in ancient Ephesus. It is seldom touched by the press and hardly can be by the pulpit for fear of offending refined taste. But refined taste, itself sometimes the offspring of this evil, must not be allowed to get up "a conspiracy of silence" which leaves inexperienced youth unwarned, and casts a veil over social vices which are sapping the foundations of society. Can this subject be discussed with such delicacy and care as to do good and not harm? I believe it can, because I believe in the Word of God. There is no other vice in regard to which the Bible speaks with such fullness and explicitness of language as that of licentiousness. One reason is because there is no other vice to which human life, in the church and out of it, is so subtly and constantly tempted, or which is so destructive to moral character. Jesus Christ spoke out on this subject to Christians not only with infinite wisdom, but with terrible plainness. The obvious reason for this is that Christian character does not consist in a fair exterior. There may be licentiousness of the mind, which is fatal to all morals, while clean thoughts, pure imaginations, are always fundamental to Christian life. The supreme Beatitude is, " Blessed are the pure in heart, for they shall see God." A religion which only restrains from overt acts of vice, and does not purify the imagination, and sanctify the secret thoughts is false. Salvation itself is moral cleanness. Hence Christ, in his sublime fidelity to his disciples, uttered that statement, which in every generation blanches the face of man: "I say unto you that whosoever looketh on a woman to lust after her hath committed adultery with her already in his heart." The sin that damns men lies in the secret thoughts of the mind. The mind of man is the man himself—the whole of him. The mind is the immortal part which is to share God's immortality. A fair outside and a corrupt mind is a whited sepulcher. No wonder God '■ desires truth in the inward parts." No wonder the man of God cried, "Cleanse me from hidden faults."

But the principal reason for speaking to young Christians on this subject is not that they intentionally give way to the temptation to social vice, but that so many, unwittingly, fall into the blunder of exposing themselves to certain forms of its danger for what they consider a justifiable reason. Thousands of young men, especially, expose themselves to fatal social perils, in order, as they claim, to broaden their experience, and give them a larger knowledge of the world. They persuade themselves that it is important even for Christians to see more of the world; that they ought to witness for themselves some of the forms of depravity of which they hear, and which they are to fight. Thus sometimes, with a good motive perhaps, but more often from a mere prurient curiosity, and always with an utterly false judgment, they venture, as mere eye-witnesses, into places of dissipation and infamy where no Christian ought to go. And because they are only well-meaning spectators, seeking a knowledge of the world, and escape without overt act of sin themselves, they think they receive no harm. This is a fatal mistake. And it is not so unusual a thing even among very respectable young men, as many good people hope and believe.

The writer had his eyes opened to this fact not long ago, by a conversation with a young man who had spent the summer in Europe. He belonged to a good church-going family in one of the Atlantic States. I think he was not a church member, but an upright, moral young man. He stated with an air of superior experience that while in Paris he "determined to see the very worst as well as the best of that city," and he did. He sought out three or four other young men, and they visited together the most fashionable and the most debased places of infamy. He stoutly affirmed that he went simply to gain a knowledge of the world, with no foul intention, and committed no criminal act; and I believe he told the truth. After describing in cold blood the unreportable things he saw and heard among the degraded women, his closing reflection was that his experience had made him almost "lose faith in womankind." At this my soul was on fire with indignation. I said to him:

"Did it ever occur to you to lose faith in yourself? You go to that most licentious city on the globe, you choose certain companions, you mistake a prurient curiosity for a better motive, you smell out those hells of nastiness where poor women, by slow degrees, and through the aggressive sin of men have sunk to the lowest pit; you visit them, see and learn all that there is, and come away very virtuous, to tell of your superior experience to other men, young and old, who are thus contaminated and tempted by your knowledge; and the result is that most of them will 'lose faith in woman,' as you did. You have possessed yourself of secrets which you can never reveal to sister or mother, and which, if publicly known, would make you distrusted and despised by all honorable women, in that ' best society' in which you move. The truth is, the one person you should lose faith in first of all is yourself. You think it has been no damage to you. You are all wrong. You will carry a wound in your soul in the form of a tainted imagination to your grave, and every companion to whom you retail your experience, unless specially forearmed by Christ, will suffer a similar wound."

This conversation leads me to say to Christian young men, with all the energy of my being, that personal experience in vice is not necessary to the most effective warfare upon it. The motive which leads one to acquaint himself personally with social vice as a means of becoming more useful as a Christian is not of God, but of the devil. It is contrary to both Christ's precept and example. It will give you experience at the expense of spirituality. The clean soul is the soul that God can use. "Blessed are the pure in heart for they shall see God." The "heart" in the Bible means generally "mind." What I plead for here is a pure mind. It must be pure if we are to be Christians. The terrible effect of familiarity with social vice is that it taints the imagination. The imagination is one of the noblest powers of the mind. By it we rise above the things of sight, and even of reason, and hold converse with the infinite. It is extremely influential in the formation of character. But from its very nature it is more easily corrupted, and more terrible in its effects when degraded than any other faculty. It is not through reason or judgment, but through the imagination, that the tempter generally comes. Seduce the imagination and the light of the soul goes out. Many persons with fair exterior indulge in forming imaginary pictures, the reality of which would be crime. The very passing of a base imagination through the mind leaves a stain which cannot be effaced on earth. For memory always cooperates with imagination and reproduces and dwells on the debasing thought, or disgusting sight, or licentious phrase, till its pollution is perpetuated in the soul. Then, no time, nor place, nor occupation is] too sacred to be intruded upon by such infernal fancies. The very sanctuary of God is not exempt. Hence the gospel too often falls on listless ears and a torpid moral nature. The very temple of the immortal mind becomes polluted.

No wonder God desires truth in the inward parts. No wonder he insists in his redemptive work upon "temperance," chastity, self-control, the dominion of reason and conscience over the passions and affections. Think what a value God sets upon the mind. He made it in his own image, for high and holy uses. But see what it becomes when corrupted imagination takes the throne. See how the moral sensibilities shrivel and die. See how fine mental powers become crippled and the spiritual life blasted in the bud. See how many a man simply by opening " eye gate" and "ear gate," as that young man did in Paris, to the allurements of the flesh, changes a noble intellectual endowment into a kennel of unclean thoughts which are not fit to be uttered anywhere but in hell.

Nothing clouds and deadens the moral sense, and therefore nothing defeats the gospel of life in the unconverted, and nothing will sooner kill all spiritual energy in a church member than the habit of licentious thoughts.

We sometimes wonder what ails certain outwardly moral young men that they do not lay hold of the gospel. Ah! The worst thing possible is the matter. A worm is at the root of the character. They have exposed their sensitive souls through "eye gate" and "ear gate" to polluting sights and sounds, and have become the victims of a tainted imagination. That is not all. The pollution of the mind is contagious. The minds of young men, in the church and out of it, are constantly coming into contact with each other. One corrupted imagination in a community of young people is a menace to the whole.

While returning from England last summer when we were about in the middle of the Atlantic, the attention of all on board was arrested by some great black object on the sea. As we drew nearer, it proved to be an old huge hulk of a vessel, apparently capsized and utterly wrecked, no rudder, no sail, no anchor, no sign of life. Where or when it was wrecked, or who once owned it, or what was its cargo, or what had become of its crew, n y one could tell. There it was, alone and desolate, but eloquently suggestive, in mid-ocean. No shore within reach to be drifted to, no haven to enter, no rest from the eternal agitation of the deep. Once a thing of beauty, almost a thing of life; now a black, helpless thing, swinging and heaving, and tossing, and dashing, and drifting, night and day, day and night, through the weeks and months, and years, at the mercy of the merciless waves. I am told that there are many such floating in the sea, never getting very far away from where they were wrecked, but drifting about in the general pathway of navigation, and that they are a source of serious danger to vessels by coming into collision with them in the night.

THE BEASTS OF EPHESUS

This impressed me very profoundly, for it set me to thinking of certain human souls out on the sea of life; souls made for noble purposes and high ends, but wrecked, spiritually drifting, never far from the place where they were wrecked, but always in the line of human life, and inexpressibly dangerous to other unsuspecting souls. In the sphere of moral influence there is nothing more to be dreaded by young people than a polluted soul, moving about in society, boasting of a superior knowledge of the world and communicating the contagion of its tainted imagination to the young men or maidens who are as yet only beginners in the Christian life. We need to shun them as we would shun the pestilence, to flee from them as we would flee from the avenger of blood. Let the divine prayer, "Lead us not into temptation, but deliver us from evil," be daily on our lips. Let us have done with that Satanic argument that young Christians should expose themselves to the contagion of social impurity for the purpose of enlarging their experience of the world. No man has any right to tempt himself and God in that way. Let us keep the immortal mind morally clean, and God will use the experience we have.

The dangerous tendency to which I have referred, is greatly enhanced by the fearfully low standard of public opinion, especially as to masculine virtue. It would seem as if the powers of darkness had formed an infernal conspiracy to corrupt the bodies and souls of the race. I refer to the double standard of morals by which public opinion estimates men and women in this matter. It seems to be everywhere taken for granted in society and even in courts of law, that social impurity is but a trifling offense in men, but an unpardonable crime in women. Equally guilty before God, society forgives and condones the crime of the man, and condemns the woman to infamy. This has two terrible results: on one hand, it encourages men in guilty self-indulgence, setting a premium on aggressive masculine solicitations; on the other, it throws the whole responsibility of the defense of social virtue on the woman, and yet it is equally fraught with moral death to both. It makes the one an outcast, the other a whited sepulcher. No more accursed sentiment ever prevailed on earth. God speed the Christianization of public opinion, "till both in theory and in practice it shall recognize the fundamental truth that the essence of right and wrong is in no way dependent on sex, and shall demand of men the same chastity as it demands of women."

The great want in both young and old Christians is a living conscience. When God made the mountains of New Hampshire, he made them largely of granite. He made them very beautiful. They are cut and crossed by ravines which contain soil enough to support trees and plants that gives picturesqueness to the outline. They are covered with patches of green in spring, and reaches of scarlet flame in autumn, and even the little mountain flower finds its place on their sides in summer. But that which sustains all this wealth of beauty and grandeur is the granite that lies below. So with Christian character. That which sustains and makes all sorts of moral beauty possible, is the granite of the soul; an enlightened, developed, tender, Christ-smitten conscience. Without that the whole fabric will collapse. What is the matter with public sentiment, nay, with our church life, on this question of masculine social purity? It is the want of the granite of character, a holy conscience, which makes men even more loyal to secret honor than to public reputation; conscience that will make a man realize that his thoughts must be as pure as the thoughts of Christ, if he is to be a Christian at all; that he stands day and night in the presence of God; that his body is the temple of the Holy Ghost; and that will make society brand the sinning man with the same stigma that it puts upon the sinning woman. To realize such a conscience and to emphasize the belief in the duty and capacity of every man to so think pure thoughts as to reflect the divine image in which he was made, Christian souls must feed, not on the popular novel, not on the Sunday newspaper, but on the Word of God.

It is wonderful how a little Bible truth clears the moral atmosphere, blows away the sophistries of public sentiment, and girds up the "loins of the mind." -\Let all tempted young men commit to memory and daily repeat to themselves such words as these: "Remove thy way far from the strange woman and come not nigh the door of her house, for her house inclineth unto death. She has cast down many wounded, yea, many strong men have been slain by her. Her house is the way to hell, going down to the chambers of death; none that go unto her return again, neither take they hold of the paths of life. Let not thy heart decline to her ways, lest thou mourn at last when thy flesh and thy body are consumed, and then say, How have I hated instruction and my heart despised reproof." The man of no understanding "goeth after her as an ox goeth to the slaughterer, or as a fool to the correction of the stocks. As a bird hasteth to the snare and knoweth not that it is for his life." "For this ye know, that no whoremonger or unclean person hath any inheritance in the kingdom of Christ and of God." "For without are dogs and sorcerers and whoremongers and murderers and idolaters, and whosoever loveth and maketh a lie." "The fearful, the unbelieving and the abominable and murderers and whoremongers and all liars shall have their part in the lake which burneth with fire and brimstone which is the second death." "Flee also youthful lusts, but follow righteousness, faith, charity, peace, with them that call on the Lord out of a pure heart." "Let no corrupt communication proceed out of your mouth." "Let no man say when he is tempted, 'I am tempted of God.' But every man is tempted when he is drawn away of his own lusts and enticed. Then when lust hath conceived it bringeth forth sin, and sin when it is finished bringeth forth death." "Ye have heard that it was said by them of old time, Thou shalt not commit adultery, but I say unto you, that whosoever looketh on a woman to lust after her, hath committed adultery with her already in his heart." "If thine eye offend thee, pluck it out and cast it from thee; for it is profitable for thee that one of thy members perish and not that thy whole body should be cast into hell."

"Blessed are the pure in heart, for they shall see God."

Chapter XII:
The Young Christian
and Market Infidelity

IT IS one of the marks of Divine Wisdom that Christians are neither immediately taken out of the world when converted, nor set apart to live in communities by themselves. Their great change is inward and spiritual, a change of aim and motive, while their social and secular relations remain substantially the same. Christians and non-Christians are in constant contact, and that contact is so close and intimate that it cannot be otherwise than momentous to both. This intermingling of converted and unconverted souls, this clash of Christian faith with Market Unbelief, in the family, the store, the railway train, and the street, works both ways. It has its advantages and its perils. The tendency is to reduce life to a common level. Hence the frequently depressed condition of the church. This does not imply that each necessarily adopts the other's views, but only that they tend to encroach upon and modify each other.

By Market Infidelity I mean that which we see and hear on the street, in the caucus, in shops and factories, and in the market-place, as distinguished from scientific or philosophical unbelief. It is the infidelity of the mouth and of the pocket rather than of the brain. It is that which is sold to the populace or to a lecture bureau for $200 a night by certain men who want to make fun of their mother's faith. Now this kind is far more difficult to resist than scientific unbelief. The fact that one rejects its statements does not remove its influence. It is like the malaria in our valleys; it is in the air; it comes to us without leave. To try to argue it down is like arguing down the Aurora Borealis. It comes most insinuatingly, at that critical and tremendously serious transitional period of life when a young Christian is passing, in his religious experience, from a faith which has till now rightly rested on the testimony of parents and teachers to intelligent convictions of his own.

I gladly concede that young Christians very seldom so far adopt infidel views as to abandon Christ. Nevertheless their faith is almost unconsciously modified; the tone of their spiritual life is lowered, and their courageous, aggressive usefulness is reduced, by the depressing atmosphere in which they live.

Now, one secret of the power of this Market Infidelity is its universality. It is everywhere, and everywhere vociferous. The secular editor prints it for the million. The genteel, but godless, business man trades in it. The Sabbath-breaker exalts it. The saloon-keeper preaches it. The debauchee enjoys it. The fashionable club man chooses it. The ward politician insinuates it. The long-haired and sad-faced sage, who still reads Paine and goes to hear Ingersoll, expounds it. The disappointed woman throws into it the charm of a beautiful sentiment. The smug and dapper youth who annexes his cap to the back of his head and wears bangs like a girl, talks it with the confidence of a philosopher. The whole mass of non-churchgoers practice it, and all half-converted, worldly-minded church members, who are settled on their lees, and are saying with the deists of Zephaniah's time, that "The Lord will not do good, neither will he do evil," are lending it their indorsement. It is plain that however earnestly young Christians may repudiate these views theoretically, it is hardly in human nature not to be practically modified by them. We cannot avoid the marketplace if we would, and it is not God's plan that we should. There is no escape from injury except by some divine fortification within.

A second element of the power of the Market Infidelity is its positive and repeated claim to be new and fresh, the product of "modern thought." It is assumed that modern thought has pulverized the old faiths; that this popular skepticism is the child of a superior light, a wiser culture or a more scientific spirit which has arisen in these later days. It says that human nature is sufficient of itself; that all it needs is scientific development; that it is now discovered that there is no need of supernatural revelation from God, and if we did need it, it would be impossible to get it.

Now, we run no risk in saying that nearly all of the multitudinous phases of modern infidelity, which the masses are repeating today, instead of being new, or the results of modern thought, are absolutely nothing but the galvanized ghosts of skeptical doctrines which were slain by the Christian fathers in the time of the Roman Empire, during the first three and a half centuries of the church. Some of these modern forms of unbelief, as for example, the deism of the seventeenth and eighteenth centuries in England, and which admits that there is a God but denies that he has anything to do with human affairs, is found distinctly stated, as we have seen, in Zephaniah's time, 630 years before Christ. That is not very new! It was thought that Hume's argument against miracles was new, but Samuel Johnson, referring to the subject said, "If I could have allowed myself to gratify my vanity at the expense of truth, what fame might I have acquired. Everything that Hume has written against Christianity had passed through my mind long before he wrote." The whole field of unevangelical humanitarianism in regard to the person of Christ, and of Agnosticism which rejected the Old Testament, and talked about the "mistakes of Moses," as well as the Rationalism which denied both the need and the possibility of a supernatural revelation from God, was fought over in the early church, and the infidel arguments of both Jews and pagans put to silence. When the same ghostly arguments were resurrected after the Protestant Reformation, under the name of the Deism of Lord Herbert and later as Materialism, they received a death-blow, a second time, from Butler and Paley on the one hand and Whitfield and Wesley on the other. The claim that the skepticism which is influencing young Christians today is the result of scientific progress, or is in any radical sense new, is simply a denial of history. The Rationalists and Materialists who are fighting the gospel today, are wielding the broken and cast-off weapons of defeated paganism. In the words of Bancroft, "Infidelity gains the victory when she wrestles with hypocrisy or with superstition, but never when her antagonist is reason."

A third element of the influence of Market Infidelity is its persistency and its confidence in reiteration after its logical basis is gone. The vast majority of people are not aware that these skeptical notions have ever been met and vanquished by Christian apologists in former ages. The Christian arguments have not been sufficiently popularized. The Market Skepticism sounds like something new in each generation, and the constant parading of dead things in new dresses, and declaring that they are alive and modern, does affect many minds by the sheer sublimity of impudence and the momentum of ignorance.

A fourth secret of this influence over Christian minds, is its resort to ridicule and scorn, and the statement of half-truths, which can easily be made the butt of a jest. A man of wit may outrage history and talk nonsense day and night, but if he can raise a popular laugh at an opponent he gains a certain victory. Lucian, the great scoffer of antiquity, did substantially what scoffers are doing today. He said faith in Christ, whom he called the " Crucified Sophist," was "one of the absurd follies of the times." Any man who can use the weapon of irony or ridicule and can laugh heartily himself, even when others see nothing indubitably funny, may be a very effective opponent of the gospel. A coarse laugh, raised by a jest aimed at the church or Bible, needs neither argument nor intelligence to produce an effect on young minds, Distortion of truth is always a very effective mode of intellectual warfare. You can disfigure the face of a friend beyond all recognition by a few crayon strokes judiciously distributed. In the same way a great truth may be disguised so as to appear both ugly and incredible. This is the stock in trade of the great American caricaturist of Christian truth, the modern imitation of Lucian, in our own generation. Mr. Nast distorting the face of a political opponent during a heated campaign, is modesty and accuracy itself, compared with the tongue of Mr. Ingersoll in disfiguring Christian truth.

If we turn now from these influences which perpetually assail the Christian life, to some of the safeguards against them, it will be well in the first place to bear in mind that the effect which Market Infidelity produces is generally not a change of conviction which undermines faith, but only a discouraging impression which cools the ardor of activity and cuts the nerve of spiritual pluck and energy. As to the real grounds of faith, we need have no fear. Scientific or philosophical unbelief has too often changed its base and so revealed its weakness to cause any alarm. Defeated as pagan denial, it shifted its ground to more philosophical Rationalism in the early church. Routed there, it changed its form after the Reformation to Deism; from Deism in England, to Atheism in France, and Pantheism in Germany; from Pantheism back to Materialism; from Materialism to revived Rationalism, and last of all, to Agnosticism, its latest form and largest concession. In each age it has repudiated the position of the preceding, and struggled for a new attitude or a new form, without altering the substance of the controversy. On the other hand, Christianity has steadily advanced along the whole line, by unwaveringly holding the position with which it began, in the defense and reassertion of the Supernatural. This shifting of position on the one side, and steadfastness on the other, through the ages, on the one essential point of discussion, shows the weakness of skepticism and the invincibleness of the Christian faith in the arena of scholarly debate. While this is true, we need not be discouraged by the unbelief of the populace, whose only want is that of a new heart. As we are not to judge of the healthfulness of a city by the atmosphere of its sewers, so neither are we to judge of the truth of a supernatural revelation by the ranting of the theater or the wrangle of the market place.

It is well, also, to remember that just as Deism, both in Old Testament times and in the days of the English Restoration, arose from a decline of morals, so all practical infidelity springs from the same source: the "evil heart of unbelief," and the presence of an unspiritual state of mind.

There is a third fact which no Christian can afford to overlook. The final resort in reassuring our hearts against the influence of practical skepticism, must be to what Christ is to us personally. The supreme appeal is to experience; that is, to our own hearts. We must have convictions of our own, born not simply out of books, or resting on the testimony of others, but born out of our personal experience with Christ. If you are conscious that Christ has emancipated you, comforted you, made a different man or woman of you, set you to loving souls and denying self for others, and hungering and thirsting for righteousness, then you can laugh at and pity all the forms of Market Infidelity. But if this personal experience is lacking, then the shallowest skepticism of the street will overthrow you. To secure, this fortification within, let there be a noble, earnest struggle with your own heart. It may cost you the slaying of self, the sacrificing of old prejudices which are very dear. Never mind. Go about it with a humble but profound purpose. The essential safeguard against all malign influences which are aimed at Christianity must be what you are yourself as the result of God's love in Jesus Christ.

Another prime safeguard to spiritual life is, in making our welfare offensive instead of defensive. The business of the Christian is not self-defense but attack. Our position, either as to faith or practice, must not be dictated by the word. No Christian soul succeeds on the Geo. B. McClelland policy. The market place is where we are to do our work. The chance which bad men get at our faith is precisely what gives us a chance at their infidelity. And "greater is he that is in you than he that is in the world." Go to your friends of Market Unbelief, directly, for purposes of conquest. To this end God has mercifully left you and the skeptic in daily contact with each other. Try to realize the omnipotence of a pure and holy life, the value of an aggressive faith, and of loving words and deeds, to these millions of the world's market place, on whom Christ had compassion, and who are really going to conquer you unless you can save them. Try to get them in love with God, for they cannot stop injuring your life till they stop hurting themselves, and they cannot stop hurting either you or themselves till they stop wronging God. Bear in mind, too, that there never was a time in the world's history when Christians had so much reason to agree with Paul when he said, "I am not ashamed of the gospel of Christ." There never was a day since the crucifixion of Christ when the gospel was so much master of the situation as it is today. There never was a time when Christian young men had so much reason for rejoicing in their faith, and so little reason for being ashamed of the Christian Church. There never was a time when so much profound scholarship was engaged in the defense and propagation of Christianity. There never was a time when the colleges of the country stood so solidly for Christian faith, or when so large a percentage of students were members of the Christian Church. More than fifty-five percentage of the thirty-four thousand college students of the United States are members of evangelical churches; and the per-cent, is increasing every year. No doubt the churches are imperfect and living below the Savior's ideal; but it is safe to say, never since the days of Paul has there been so great an awakening among Christians as to their duty to the poor, as to the rooting out of the spirit of caste, as to the universal brotherhood of man, as to a more Christian political economy, as to the conversion of the heathen, and as to real sympathy with the needs and struggles and aspirations of young men, as there is today. Indeed, the peculiar characteristic of this generation is the sympathy of the churches with the young. We cannot deny that there are reasons for some of the slurs of market skepticism in regard to church life. But this splendid awakening of the last few years to active cooperation with Young Men's Christian Association work, with Christian Endeavor work, with all reasonable Christian socialism and with almost every high reform that fires the imagination and engages the energies of young people, demonstrates both the purpose and fitness of the church to save mankind. It never was more efficient and was never more needed than today.

Chapter XIII:
The Young Christian
and the Majority

ONE OF the wiliest beasts that Paul had to fight at Ephesus was the mighty force of numbers, the sweep and momentum of public opinion. When he began his work in that city, there was there a little obscure band of Christians which might have been counted upon the fingers of your hands. The great, teeming, busy city was all against him. He had to face the historic prejudices of the half-savage, hungry, hirsute mob of the masses of the poor; he had to face the Pharisaic pride of the Jewish Colony; he had to face the more intelligent and more selfish followers of Demetrius, whose shrewd cry was, "Sirs, ye know that by this craft we have our wealth;" he had to face the contempt of the wealthy and luxurious, who set the fashions for Asia Minor, and controlled the public sentiment of the state; he had to face the abhorrence of the devout worshipers of Diana, and the derision of the philosophers, and the contempt of literary men. Added to all these was the city's pride of learning, its pride of culture, its pride of civilization, the influence of its hoary superstitions, its vast history, its splendor of wealth, the awful momentum of its corruptions, its lusts, and its life of pleasure, without hope and without God. All this added weight and solidity to the majority against Paul. Paul on the other hand was poor, obscure, alone—one man against the world. How easy to acquiesce in public sentiment and to say,

"The fight is a hopeless one." But no, inspired by the spirit of the Nazarene, he resisted the majority and preached nonconformity, till his voice has been heard in every age and clime. The same battle has to be fought, in one form or another, by every Christian today. The Bible constantly reminds us that the cause of Christ is in the minority still. A great part of the Christian warfare consists in resisting the majority. The vast bulk of the wealth, the power, the numbers of the world, has been against spiritual life from the beginning. Numerically, Christ's followers still occupy but a small portion of the earth. Christians are everywhere reminded that, as the world goes, they belong to a small minority; that they must make up their minds to face that fact when they identify themselves with Christ. They must expect, not only no sympathy from the outside world in their spiritual endeavors, but rather, in one form or another, active opposition.

We are also reminded in a thousand different ways that the force of numbers is a tremendous force to antagonize. Public sentiment is well nigh resistless, not because it aims directly to destroy spiritual life, but because it aims only to secure conformity. Hence the subtle power of the multitude. For this reason the whole weight of the Word of God is thrown against conformity. We are to resist the world. We are forbidden to follow the multitude. We are to come out and be separate. We are to be transformed by the renewing of our minds, that we may prove (to the world itself) "what is that good and acceptable and perfect will of God." The spiritual conflict of life is always along the line of non-conformity. Power, victory, salvation, lie along that line. The working Christian has simply to make up his mind to join the minority and fling himself into the battle. Anyone who will analyze the influence of numbers especially on younger minds, will see that resistance is no child's play.

1. There is a strange and subtle fascination about numbers, which tends to blind the mind to the sense of sin and danger. How much more natural and agreeable it seems to go in the way the multitude are going. How much more confidence one has in his own position, when he sees that he is one of a great company. Tell him he is on the wrong road, and his heart, if not his head, will reply, "It cannot be, I am not alone. Here are the rich and the poor, the learned and the ignorant. Here is much of the best culture and learning of the ages. Here, too, are the young, the fair, the jubilant—all with me. It cannot be that this great busy, joyous company is going to the bad." Sin loses its ugly look when committed by a majority. Individual responsibility becomes lost in the sense of the crowd. A man in a mob, burning or killing his fellow man, never feels the same sense of guilt that he would if he undertook the deed alone. Nevertheless we read that, "though hand join in hand, the wicked shall not go unpunished."

2. The force of numbers tends to exalt the idea of *reputation* above that of character. Conformity to the multitude seems all-important; to be singular looks like conceit or madness. The popular, respectable thing is conformity. It is this that makes moral reform so difficult and the progress of Christ's kingdom so slow. Throw yourself into any cause that is unpopular, and all the Beasts which Paul had to fight will come at you, each according to its nature—hissing, howling, barking, resisting all change, till your cause perchance happens to fight its way to popularity. Then they take it up and claim it as their own.

3. The influence of the majority, from the nature of the case, is on the side of what is, rather than what *ought to be*. The established order of things, especially if it be the growth of years, is regarded as sacred. Hence arises intolerance, persecution, the inquisition, the fagot and the stake.

4. The influence of the multitude pressing constantly for conformity obscures the fact that in the highest concerns of existence *the whole unconverted world is wrong*. Hence the influence of the majority keeps our eyes blinded to the fundamental fact of the Gospel, that the world at large is against God, and hence that the moment Christ came into the world he had to begin a warfare of non-conformity.

5. This indirect influence of the majority tends to enthrone fashion, which is only another name for conformity. It thus makes spiritual progress hard, uphill work. The tendency of society is toward a common level. The majority destroys moral courage, makes men shrink from what the crowd calls "fanaticism" or "ultraism." The result is, that the spirit of independent thought and self-denial is crushed. Take the socialistic reform of today. Thousands of us content ourselves too long with simply denouncing the restless agitation of the poor, without attempting to investigate or expose the causes of complaint. Take the temperance reform. Thirty years ago it was said, "The pinch of the temperance reformation has not yet been decided. That pinch will come when we reach the question whether we will really exercise *self-denial* in order to crush the evil." The pinch in our own day is to come when Christian people, as such, are put to the test whether they will actually stand up and say, "God helping us, whether popular or unpopular, we will help defeat any man, to

whatever party he may belong, who does not work openly for the destruction of the saloon, and we will help elect the best men, to whatever party they belong, who *are* sincerely working against the saloon." When the church of Christ makes up its mind to do for the cause of temperance just what the liquor oligarchy is doing for the rum traffic—that is refuse to tie itself up to any organization under the sky—when it binds itself only to right men and right principles rather than to parties, and holds itself free to move from side to side and ready to cast the weight of its concentrated influence in favor of any movement which refuses to ally itself with the evil to be overthrown, then it will hold the balance of power in the nation as the liquor men hold it now. The church of Jesus Christ, with its ten millions of members, if good for anything, *ought* to hold the balance of power in this nation.

6. Following the multitude leads to extravagance of living, to selfish waste of money, to secularism and materialism on the part of Christians; and that robs the church of its power to help the world. It blots out the distinction between Christian and worldling. It puts all on practically the same level, just as did the wretched evil of the state church in early New England, and as the state church is still doing on the Continent of Europe today.

Now if there is anything with regard to which the Word of God is clear and imperative, it is that Christians, for their own sake, and for the sake of the world, must refuse to follow the multitude. The Bible is full of remarkable examples, of both the right and the wrong kind, which bear upon this point. A pertinent one of the evil kind is given in the case of Aaron when he followed the lead of the majority and made the golden calf. Standing as a representative of God among men, he meanly yielded to the capricious sentiment of the multitude when he ought to have met it with a counter sentiment which belonged to, and was worthy of, all the ages. Head of the priesthood as he was, he forsook God and yielded to the public sentiment of the hour, and then in his lame and miserable apology, laid the blame on the people. The effect on the man himself, on the multitude, on the cause of righteousness, was simply disastrous. A prompt rebuke, a kindly and cogent argument, a little light given to the people from any heroic man of God would have averted that terrible sin of apostasy. Unaccountably soon, he and the people alike" lost sight of their great spiritual mission and the cause of God was set back.

How noble, how heroic, how promotive of all righteousness, was the conduct of Moses, the real man of God, when he came down from the mount and found what was done. Against his own brother, in the face of the multitude, in defiance of public opinion Moses said, "What did this people unto thee that thou hast brought this great sin upon them?" "Who is on the Lord's side. Let him come unto me. Draw your swords; consecrate yourselves to the Lord, every man upon his son and upon his brother; that the Lord may bestow a blessing upon you this day." "Oh, this people have sinned a great sin!" This was the heroic surgery that saved the Jewish church for the ages. It is a similar spirit that must save humanity today.

Erasmus saw the needs of the church and the world as clearly as Luther, but he would not risk the personal discomfort and danger of unpopularity and persecution involved in opposing the majority, and he threw away a sublime opportunity. Luther, of a different type, faced the multitude, went to the Diet at Worms, and made the Reformation. Pilate saw the innocence of Jesus and the injustice of his enemies as clearly as we do, but he could not face public opinion. Jesus was in the minority. He had a small, unpopular backing. Pilate had ends of his own to serve, and he gave Jesus to the mob. On the other hand, the whole of Christ's own gracious and divine life was one sublime refusal to follow the multitude. At first he stood alone without a friend or party. Then he cast in his lot with poor fishermen and publicans, and only a dozen of them at that, and stood against all the force of numbers, all the might of hoary customs, all the strength of traditions, all the pride of caste and culture, all the scorn, even of the rabble, though it led him to the cross. But he thereby purchased redemption for the world. At the moral heat of that one holy life, all consecrated men and women, from that day to this, have kindled their heroic fires. Old and young, rich and poor, ignorant and learned alike, have risen up, one after another, through the years, in the strength of that example, and said, "I, too, can refuse to follow the multitude to do evil." And here alone lies the hope of man.

In the strength of that principle, and inspired by that life Stephen faced the Sanhedrin, John faced Patmos, and Paul met Nero. In the light of that one Divine Example, God's martyr men and women stood firm and radiant when the fires of the Roman Empire and of the later inquisition were kindled under their feet. They would not conform to majorities, for, like Stephen, they looked up and saw Jesus on the right hand of God.

Oh, for such men today, especially young men, at the bar, in the editor's chair, in the store, in the workshop, in the pulpits of every city, and in the halls of legislation —

to champion the suffering cause of temperance, to plead for the working-man's Sabbath of rest, to herald a new political economy, to raise the standard of the church, to fight the Beast of Conformity to the World.

Chapter XIV:
The Young Christian
and the Weed

*"But tobacco, tobacco—what a rude crowbar is that with
which to pry into the delicate tissues of the brain."*
—Emerson.

BUT WHY discuss the tobacco question? Why attack the
smoking habit, when, according to its advocates, it soothes
and exhilarates, promotes sociability, is the solace of rich
and poor alike, and is enjoyed by the greater part of the
male population of the world? Is it not simply butting one's
head against the Chinese wall to oppose an evil, if it be
an evil, from which the government draws an immense
revenue, in which millions are invested, and which the
practice of the minister, the lawyer, the doctor, the begger
man and the thief universally sustains?

The main reasons for discussing the subject must
appear as we proceed, but this much may be stated here.
The importance of the theme calls for discussion. The
universality of the use of tobacco, the ease with which
it becomes a master and a tyrant; the mad avidity with
which all classes, ages and ranks acquire the habit, certainly indicates to thoughtful people that tobacco has
some remarkable influence on the human system. This
of itself clothes the subject with significance. Another
reason is the tremendous rapidity of the spread of the habit
in the nation and the world. Still another, is the right of

self-protection for those who do not believe in its use, or enjoy its fumes. Moreover, if there is even a well-grounded suspicion that the tobacco habit is hurtful to men, and hostile to the spread of the Gospel of Christ, that itself is sufficient reason for the agitation of the theme.

It may seem to some like fanaticism to grapple with an evil based upon almost universal custom and backed by such enormous money interests Indeed, it looks as if such an evil must have come to stay. But to the Christian the only thing that has really come to stay is the Kingdom of God; and if that stays, I, for one, believe that the tobacco habit must ultimately go. The hopelessness of the outlook may be only the result of unchristian timidity. "Truth has no greater foe than the distrust of some of its friends in its power." I think it is Dr. Lieber who, speaking of nations, says that some are above and others are below the lines of agitation of great subjects. The same is true of individuals. We were all below the line of the agitation of the temperance question, seventy-five years ago. Some people are below the line of religious doubt and unrest simply for want of mental and moral awakening; others are above it, having grappled with their doubts and settled them. So, perhaps> multitudes are below the line of agitation of the tobacco problem, but it will not be so forever. It cannot be denied that tobacco is a great leveler. It brings the churches and the slums, the preacher, the tramp, and the debauchee into the same fraternity, in this one particular at least. If, therefore, the churches cannot consistently criticize the slums in this matter, it may be worth while to agitate the subject and see why.

THE BEASTS OF EPHESUS

THE GREAT BOON.

Now the first thing that occurs to one looking at the enormous consumption of the weed, and the arguments of its defenders, is a feeling of pity for the poor, civilized world before it got this stupendous boon from the aboriginal savages of America. What a stupid affair Christian civilization must have been before 1492! No pipes, no cigars, no snuff; nothing to put in the mouth but victuals and drink! What a miserable world socially; nothing to promote interesting conversation! What a fidgety world; nothing to calm the nerves! What commonplace thoughts; nothing to exhilarate the imagination! What a humdrum life wives must have led, before they rose to the heroic dignity of enduring the stench of their smoking husbands breath, forty years, more or less, without complaint! What gloom must have hung over the life of every young man; not a whiff of smoke to mark the progress of his rising manhood! The world must have seemed a "fleeting show" even to the little boys! And then, what did the nations do without their tobacco revenue? All life would have been a burden if Christian people had not learned of the heathen how to live. To be sure the savages of San Domingo did not do everything for us. Indeed they were woefully behind the times. They inhaled the fumes of tobacco through the same aperture in the face in which they put their snuff, namely, the nose! It was given to the Latin and especially the great Anglo-Saxon race to discover and apply the principle of taking the smoke into the mouth. Neither did we get the great principle of adulteration from the savages. That, too, is wholly a product of modern civilization. The poor heathen probably never thought of enriching their tobacco by the use of rhubarb leaves, dock, colts foot, beech, plantain, oak and elm, peat, earth, bran, sawdust, (they had no sawdust), malt, rootlets, meal of barley, oats, beans, pear, potatoes, starch and chickory leaves steeped in tar oil; all to make the business more profitable.

CONCESSIONS.

In entering upon any serious discussion of the subject, it is necessary first of all to make certain concessions.

1. In dealing with the physical effects to tobacco, there has doubtless been much exaggeration on the part of some who have opposed its use. Indeed, there may have been some lies told on both sides.

2. It must be conceded that some men have smoked through a long life and are not physically dead yet.

3. Many, even Christian people, habitually indulge this disgusting habit, and yet, cannot be charged with sin in the matter, because they have never given thought enough to the subject to put conscience on the alert. That is, their consciences are not as yet distinctively Christian in regard to that subject.

CAUSES OF RAPID SPREAD.

The tremendous rapidity with which the tobacco habit has grown upon the world, is itself a serious problem. The following are perhaps some of the causes:

1. The universal craving of nature for exhilaration, a craving which, if not kept under control of reason and conscience, crystallizes into a vice.

2. The example of leading and influential men. Sir Walter Raleigh, who did much to make the custom popu-

lar in England, "took a pipe just before going to the scaffold." If he had gone to the scaffold just before taking the pipe, England would have more reason to be proud of him.

3. The child instinct for imitation, whether of good or bad habits.

4. The subserviency of ail classes of people to fashion.

5. The passion for money and the discovery that tobacco could become a profitable article of trade. This has led manufacturers and traders to create and cultivate for the sake of personal gain, an artificial demand. Thus every man engaged in the making or selling of tobacco becomes a tempter and corrupter of his fellow men.

6. The State and National governments encouraged the traffic in and consumption of tobacco, for the sake of revenue. And so it has become part of our civilization. "Thirteen European governments have made the trade a State monopoly." The native depravity of the heart, which ever tends to corrupt our nature and break its laws, is thus amazingly aided in its downward course by the passion for gain and the exigencies of trade.

These and similar considerations may explain the universality of the vice in spite of all laws and penalties against it.

LEGAL and MORAL EFFORTS FOR ITS RESTRICTION.

Thoughtful people who have had the welfare of their fellow men at heart have always warned us against the danger of this evil. Medical and scientific testimony has accumulated against it in every generation for four hundred years, and still the habit has spread till rich and poor, old and young, ministers of Christ and servants of the devil are alike its slaves, and public sentiment scarcely ventures to raise its voice in opposition. Queen Elizabeth prohibited the use of tobacco and declared the practice a "demoralizing vice, tending to reduce her subjects to the condition of savages, whose habits they imitated." King James both taxed and prohibited tobacco. In modern times, it is well known that efforts have been made to stop the use of tobacco in schools and colleges. This has been done in France, Germany and Switzerland. Switzerland made a law in 1880 prohibiting the sale of tobacco to minors under fifteen years of age and making it an offense against the law for such to smoke. Even the Sultan of Morocco has prohibited the use of tobacco to his people, and has his prohibitory edicts read in all the mosques. The early laws of New England on this subject, though rigid in their prohibitions, indicate a low moral sense of evil, and yet they show that the danger was perceived.

In a certain provincial government of New England a law was passed forbidding "any person under twenty-one years of age, or any other that hath not already accustomed himself to the use thereof, to take any tobacco until he hath brought a certificate under the hands of some who are approved for knowledge and skill in physick, that it is useful to him and also that he hath received a lycense from the courte for the same." Again "It is ordered that no man within this coloyne, after the publication hereof, shall take any tobacko publiquely in the streett, highwayes, oranybarneyardes, or uppon training dayes, in any open places, under the penality of six pence for each offence."

In the early records of Harvard is a regulation that "No scholar shall take tobacco unless permitted by the president; with the consent of his parents, on good reasons first given by a physician, and then only in a sober and private manner."

At a town meeting at Portsmouth, N. H., 1662, it was "ordered that a cage be built, or some other means devised at the discretion of the select men, to punish such as take tobacco on the Lord's day, in time of publick service." Ten years later the town "voted that if any person shall smoke tobacco in the meeting-house during religious service, he shall pay a fine of five shillings, for the use of the town."

The old Massachusetts Colony laws provided a penalty for those who should smoke tobacco "within twenty poles of any house or shall take tobacco at any inn or victualling house, except in a private room, so that neither the master nor the guests shall take offence thereat."

In several states of the Union, in our own day, laws have been enacted prohibiting the sale of tobacco and cigars to minors. In our national schools, at West Point and Annapolis, it is well known that the weed has been repeatedly and at last successfully excluded, on both sanitary and moral grounds. The same is true of a number of Christian colleges in this country, notably of Oberlin; the American College and Education Society declines to aid men who use tobacco. The noble work of the Woman's Christian Temperance Union in securing temperance education, including both stimulants and narcotics in our public schools, is accomplishing much in the awakening of thought upon the subject and for the protection of the young. The legislature of Michigan after wide correspondence with educators and medical experts has just passed a law prohibiting the manufacture, sale or giving away of cigarettes of any form in that state. These facts indicate to some extent the awakening of the conscience of the nation on this subject, but as yet it is only the fitful tossing of the hand of the slumbering giant, who when fully awake, will surely rise and strike.

INCREASE OF PRODUCTION AND USE.

In spite of all these efforts for the restriction of the evil, it is enormously on the increase. From 1880 to 1888 there was an increase of 44 per cent, in the number of cigars used in the United States, and nearly 400 per cent, increase in the number of cigarettes. Besides this, almost two-fifths of the tobacco used in Europe is produced in this country. Professor Wallace of Michigan says: "The use of cigarettes has increased five-fold in the last three years." The tobacco bill in the United States, we are told by various writers, is larger than our bread bill. The whole cost of our National smoke is more that three hundred million dollars annually, that is, over seven times more than is paid annually for all religious purposes. In 1880 it amounted to five dollars for each man, woman and child in the country. Or for smokers alone, an average of about thirty dollars apiece, annually; which according to Dr. Sperry's calculation, would amount at six per cent., in sixty years, to about $16,000 for each smoker. In 1880, the annual production of tobacco was 462,000,000 pounds against 262,000,000 pounds, ten years before. In the city of New York alone, about 75,000,000 cigars are used annually at a cost of $9,000,000. With these facts in view, we are prepared to maintain the proposition that the tobacco habit as it is today is physically, socially, financially, mentally and morally a hurtful, dangerous, and degrading vice.

THE BEASTS OF EPHESUS

I. PHYSICALLY:—In discussing this point, it may be well, first of all, to notice the position of the one serious writer whom I have been able to find who defends the tobacco habit on what he claimed to be scientific grounds. Mr. John Fiske, M. A., 1869, took the position that "There is no physical pleasure in the long run, comparable with that which is afforded by tobacco." This is the key to his entire argument, and his conclusion is, that "it does pay to smoke." Yet even this champion admits that tobacco is a poison and not a food; that if taken in sufficient quantity it destroys life, while in less quantity it will only sicken, but in sufficiently small quantity it does not harm. He also concedes that there are some people whom the smallest quantity will injure at once, and that it is always bad for children and youth. These admissions would seem to be sufficient to lead intelligent men to give the weed a wide berth. For it is certainly difficult to restrain children from that which their elders habitually practice; and the men are but rare who observe the safe rule of moderation when once the habit becomes the master. Mr. Fiske himself while taking a cold midnight drive, smoked eight or nine large 20-cent cigars and felt that he rather overdid the matter. He compares the use of tobacco with that of common salt, both of which are poisons and destructive to life if used to excess; therefore both must be used with temperance. His fallacy here lies in the simple fact that salt, as he himself admits, is essential to human life, while tobacco is not. The rule of temperance is to be applied to foods and medicines which are essential to life and health. From poisons which have absolutely no food value and are attended with dangers in every case, the law of nature suggests total abstinence.

We may add in passing that if Mr. Fiske's argument that " there is no physical pleasure comparable to that from tobacco," is good at all, he must be a selfish and barbarous man who does not insist upon his wife and grown up children enjoying the same "incomparable pleasure." I do not understand Mr. Fiske to take this position. Indeed, there is nothing which reveals more clearly the selfish nature of the tobacco habit than the howl of derision that generally meets its indulgence by women. If it be a solace to weary heads and shattered nerves, the wives, the mothers, the needlewomen and the servant girls, who generally work thirteen hours a day, to the man's ten or twelve, have the first claim to this " incomparable pleasure."

Now it is a significant fact that nearly all the vast array of medical and scientific testimony against tobacco (only the smallest part of which I can here use), is in view of its physical effects. On this point I urge no opinion of my own, but simply the unassailable judgment of the latest science. An English medical journal, the *Scalpel*, says:

If there is a vice more prostrating to the mind and body, and more crippling to man's spiritual nature, we have yet to be convinced of it.

The journal entitled *Science*, which is an authority among scientific men, made the following utterance about a year ago:

Nicotine is one of the most powerful nerve poisons known. Its virulence is compared to that of prusic acid. It destroys life, not by attacking a few, but all the functions essential to it, beginning with the center, the heart. A significant indication of this is that there is no substance known which can counteract its effects. Its depressing action upon the heart is the most notice-able and noteworthy symptom of nicotine poisoning. The frequent existence of what is known as " smoker's heart" in men whose health is in no other respect disturbed, is due to this fact.

The same journal gives the following as a result of investigation by a Parisian Society against the use of tobacco:

In an experimental observation of thirty-eight boys of all classes of society and of average health who had been using tobacco for periods ranging from two months to two years, twenty-seven showed severe injury to the constitution and insufficient growth; thirty-two showed the existence of irregularity of the heart's action, disordered stomachs, cough and crav-ing for alcohol; thirteen had intermittency of the pulse, and one had consumption. After they had abandoned the use of tobacco,within six months' time one-half were free from all their former symptoms, and the remainder had recovered by the end of the year.

This journal also presents the following as the effect of tobacco in the deterioration of national or tribal life:

When Europeans first visited New Zealand they found in the native Maoris the most finely developed and powerful men of any of the tribes inhabiting the islands of the Pacific. Since the introduction of tobacco, for which the Maoris developed a passion-ate liking, they have, from this cause alone, it is said, become decimated in numbers and at the same time reduced in stature and in physical well-being, so as to be an altogether inferior type of men.

The *Sanitarian* for December, 1887, a magazine sustained by such men as Profs. C. R. Agnew of New York, H. L. Bowditch of Massachusetts, T. J. Turner, Medical Director of the United States Navy, and a host of other leading men, contains an article on "The Tobacco Poison," by George J. Zeigler, M. D., of Philadelphia, which Dr. J. H. Jackson of Danville, N. Y., pronounces the "most scientific and absolutely unassailable argument against the use of tobacco" he has ever seen. In this article Dr. Zeigler says:

> Tobacco so effectually deadens and destroys vital excitability and the inherent contractibility of the living tissues that it is not safe even as a drug. Tobacco poisons the blood both directly and indirectly and thereby effects injuriously every particle and part of the body.

He says further, that "twenty young men competed at Westfield, Mass., for a West Point cadetship, and the examining surgeons had to reject ten of them on account of 'tobacco heart' brought on by cigarette smoking." The same writer also holds that through the law of heredity the children of smokers, brought up in its atmosphere in infancy, are both physically and mentally injured by the influence of tobacco. He goes so far as to say that "even the unborn are deleteriously affected by it, as it often destroys them and causes premature birth; tobacco being a powerful abortifacient." "The slaughter of the innocents in tenement houses and other close places, is no doubt largely due to the poisonous action of tobacco."

Even *Cope's Tobacco Plant,* a journal of the trade, says:

Few things could be more pernicious to boys, growing youths, and persons of unformed constitution than the use of tobacco in any of its forms.

The *Medical and Surgical Reporter* quotes the following from Dr. Willard Parker of New York:

That tobacco is a poison is proved beyond question. It is now many years since my attention was called to the insidious but positively destructive effects of tobacco on the human system. I have seen a great deal of its influence on those who use it and work on it or in it. Cigar-makers, snuff-manufacturers, etc., have come under my care in hospitals and in private practice, and such persons never recover soon and in a healthy manner from any case of injury or fever. They are more apt to die in epidemics, more prone to apoplexy and paralysis. The same is true also of those who smoke or chew.

Dr. Parker further says:

I do not place my individual self in opposition to tobacco, but science in the form of physiology and hygiene is opposed to it, and science is the expression of God's will in the government of his work in the universe.

Dr. James H. Jackson, says: "I believe tobacco is sapping the moral and physical foundations of the race, more even than alcohol." Prof. W. S. Sperry of Ann Arbor, speaking of cigarette smoking, says:

It lowers vitality, it lessens bodily vigor, it unfits the victim for concentrated effort, it is always associated with a low degree of morals and is generally with the practice of other vices.

It was in view of such facts as these, gathered from a wide range of correspondence, that the committee before the Michigan Legislature the other day urged the conclusion that the increase of the habit was " alarming and that the time had come for radical legislation."

Now, for any man to defend the habit, in either old or young, in the face of this testimony of the latest scientific research, which might be quoted to the extent of a volume, is surely the blindest and most reckless infatuation; and to practice the habit without being able to defend it is an inconsistency unworthy of a man. It seems well nigh useless to enact laws to guard the young against this evil, for there is in these days no protection to anybody from the fumes of tobacco, especially in our cities, and one of the worst signs of the times is that non-smokers seem willing to tamely acquiesce in the injury offered to their health and the insult to the rights of their humanity.

II. Socially. The claim that the use of tobacco promotes sociability is the falsest and absurdest of its claims. It is equivalent to saying that the absence of cleanliness of person and sweetness of breath, the absence of pure air, the absence of women and children, the absence of bodily health, and of minds acting in the normal condition in which God made them, together with the presence of bad company and an utter disregard of the rights of others, are essential to sociability. Such a claim is a slander alike on human and divine nature. The fact is, for any man to smell strongly, is an offense against society, be he Negro or fine gentleman, and the gentleman smoker considers it so himself, if the smell be of onions, or garlic, or cabbage, or even perfumery; but by the process of tobacco-blinding, he sees no offense in his being saturated with his own favorite smell.

III. The Financial aspect of the question is not simply the vast amount of money wasted in the aggregate, though that indeed is appalling. A billion of dollars squandered every year in smoke! America, with its millions of poor, wasting more than a third of that sum! But the financial evil lies mostly where it cannot be expressed in statistics. God only knows how many poor women who already drudge like beasts of burden have to increase their toils and discomforts in order that their husbands may enjoy this unsocial and debasing luxury. God only knows how many poor children go poorly clad and fed and educated, because their fathers insist upon selfishly dividing their scanty earning between their children and their pipes. God only knows how many honest debts stand unpaid because tobacco has to be bought. God only knows how many young men are made thieves and defaulters by this selfish indulgence which is so expressive that neither their income nor their moral manhood can bear the stain.

There is no mystery about hard times for the poor. Nothing strange about boys falling into bad company under this system of enormous and wilful waste. In the financial question there is always a moral element. With Christian people especially, it can never be a question of mere personal pleasure, as to what a man shall do with his money. The human family as a whole has a claim upon him. It is not simply the poor children of smokers who suffer from his indulgence, it is also country, humanity, and "the world lying in wickedness." When every Christian and benevolent cause is suffering for money to extend the kingdom of God, it betrays a criminal ignorance of, or else a criminal indifference to, the cause of Christ, for Christian men, whether rich or poor, to waste on their own artificial appetites that which would equip all the agencies for the evangelization of the world.

Granting that it is a real pleasure to a smoker to indulge this habit, that of itself can be a decisive argument for no thoughtful man. There are surely moral considerations which must have weight. It may be a pleasure and yet a low one. It may be a high duty to give up a low pleasure because it is offensive to wife and friends, dangerous to children and injurious to health; and even if these considerations were removed, duty might require it to be given up because it cheats the family out of some necessary good. Or again, if this argument had no weight, the pleasure might still be wrong, because it prevents a man from being able to give the Gospel of Christ to the rest of the world.

The rich man may say that his cigars do not pinch his children or prevent him from giving to the Lord's cause; and at any rate that which he smokes is his own. But under our Lord's idea of stewardship I do not find that very much of a man's money really is his own. And if it were, that would not settle the question, for it is not true that every man has a right to do as he likes with his own. "He has only a right to do as he ought with his own." Nor do I see that a steward who has much entrusted to him, has any more right to consume a part of it upon his lusts than one who has but little. There are luxuries which may seem quite justifiable even to the Christian, but when humanity is in direful need, this waste through a hurtful habit is essentially selfish, and therefore absolutely unchristian,

IV. MENTALLY. It hardly needs to be said that a physical evil is also a mental one. The body and mind are so closely related that whatever injures one is hurtful to the other. Accordingly, medical and scientific men affirm that the use of tobacco impairs the memory and weakens the power of concentrating thought. An English surgeon says that the smokers and chewers, as a rule, are lacking in the fortitude necessary to undergo the surgical operations. The excessive use of this poison also produces insanity. In the General Hospital of Massachusetts, some years ago, eight cases of insanity were ascribed to the use of tobacco. ^The opposition of educators to the habit is always based, in part at least, upon its deadening effects on the mind. One point of which the testimony recently presented to the Michigan Legislature was "uniform," was that the cigarette habit deadens the mental faculties. Dr. Hammond of New York says that under the influence of tobacco, "the action of the brain is impaired. The ability to think, and in fact all mental concentration, is weakened." It is said that no tobacco user ever graduated at the head of his class in Harvard University. The same is doubtless true in other institutions. Dr. L. B. Sperry, after giving statistics of tobacco using and scholarship at Yale, says, "These facts certainly justify one or two inferences, either that the use of tobacco results as a rule in mental deterioration and inferior scholarship, or that deteriorated and inferior minds are the ones that as a rule most readily contract the custom of using the filthy narcotic." The champion of the weed can take which horn of the dilemma he pleases.

V. MORALLY. The investigation of experts agrees perfectly with the observation of men in general as to the moral effects of tobacco. "Worst of all," says Dr. Zeigler of Philadelphia, "it debases the moral as well as the mental and physical nature; perverts the conscience, induces laziness, selfishness, deceitfulness, cruelty and sensuality." Ruskin charges that it "demoralizes youth, as enabling them to pass their time happily in idleness." Dr. Howell of Lansing, Mich., says, "It destroys the moral sensibility, and leads to other vices." A close observation, by any thoughtful person, will convince him that the use of tobacco dulls the moral sense as to the rights and comforts of other people. It creates an unnatural appetite and thus becomes the stepping stone to intemperance. The man who loses his self-control in one respect is less his own master in everything. It is beyond dispute that the habit breaks the moral power of the will. There is no slavery more relentless, nor chain harder to break. Even the appetite of the drunkard is more easily overcome. I have a friend who daily deplores this bondage into which he has fallen, but lacking the moral power to throw away his pipe, has often in desperation put his tobacco into the hands of his wife. After a few days of abstinence he becomes so restless, so woebegone, so ill, so almost inhuman that the poor wife, who by this selfish arrangement is made to bear all the strain, relents, and returns the pipe to her husband, who is still a slave to the habit. Another friend says it would deliberately kill him to give up his tobacco. General Grant broke the habit of drink, and admitting that tobacco injured him, promised a friend to give it up; but even his iron will was too much crippled, and he died at last the victim of the cigar. This is a slavery which its own victims nearly all deplore. Fathers while setting the bad example warn their children against it. The father who should train his son to smoke or chew would be considered a monster, and yet every parent who indulges in the habit is indirectly guilty of that sin. Let him preach as he may, his example is tenfold more powerful than his precept.

L. B. Sperry, M. D., lecturing recently before the students of Oberlin College on the subject of tobacco, concluded his address with the following arraignment of the weed. I cannot do better at this point of the argument than to quote his words. He says: "In the court of scientific appeal and of Christian equity I find registered eight indictments against tobacco:

1. It impoverishes and exhausts the soil upon which it is raised more than any other crop that we cultivate.

2. Its use is expensive to all who indulge in it; actually impoverishing many and often depriving their families of the comforts and even of the necessaries of life.

3. Its use in any form or place is a filthy practice on the part of its devotees, and its use in public is an offense and many times even an insult to those who do not use it.

4. It is physically unhealthy, not only to those who use it, but to those who by association are subjected to its influences.

5. It injures the mental power and balance of its victim, dulling and deteriorating the intellect, the emotions and the will.

6. It demoralizes and despiritualizes to some extent all who use it in any form.

7. Its general public use blunts the public moral sense, degrading not only the individual habitue, but also society at large.

8. Its degenerating effects, physical, mental, moral and spiritual, through the forces of heredity, are increasingly

felt by succeeding generations. Its use tends to destroy the race.

Tobacco, like all other narcotics as used by the masses, is a blight and a curse, the devil's pet agency, at once an enchantment and a scourge. It is really useful only for killing pestiferous insects."

CONCLUSION

What then is to be done? What can Christian philanthropy do about it?

1. Agitate. Cease to quietly acquiesce and begin everywhere to discuss the evil, so that it shall be forever after impossible for good men to fall into this bondage ignorantly. This is God's method in all moral reforms. Throw light on the mature and tendencies of the habit. Apply the Gospel of Christ. While conceding that the habit may not be a sin to those who don't know any better, it is safe to say that it may be a sin for Christian people not to think about it and get all the light they can. The thoughtless adoption of any habit by a whole people is no proof that it is right or safe. Little or nothing can be accomplished as yet by law. The moral sense must be awakened. Our stronghold is to stand by the laws of nature and the laws of God. Women must make their influence felt in this matter. If they do not believe in tobacco at all, they ought to say so with an emphasis. When young ladies fully commit themselves against any social and degrading custom, especially among young men, that custom will begin to disappear. We hear much in these days about woman's rights, and I believe in woman's rights. She certainly has the right, among many other things, to noble companionship and pure air, and it would be a very encouraging sign to see

her assert it. But when we see a woman willing to train her children in the blue atmosphere of tobacco smoke without a protest, or when we see a young lady walking or riding with a young man who wears a pipe or a cigar in his teeth, and that young lady is willing to swallow the vile fumes that come from his mouth, simply for the infinitesimal privilege of his company, I say, there is a woman, there is a girl, who does not believe in woman's rights. She may believe in voting, very likely she does, but she cares little or nothing for woman's rights or woman's duties either.

2. The holy principles of the Gospel which aim to free men from all forms of bondage can never be fully applied to human life when this habit prevails. The kingdom of God cannot fully come, till this goes. It is well known that the moral instinct of every man makes the defiler of the temple a criminal; and that instinct is but the shadow of God's appreciation of holiness. The temple is sacred. Now the apostle, by a noble figure of speech, transfers the idea of the temple to the regenerate soul. "Ye are the temple of God and the spirit of God dwelleth in you. What, know ye not that your bodies are the temple of the Holy Ghost?" The renewed mind is the work of the Holy Spirit. It is the seat of the operations of the Spirit on the earth. It is dear to God.

Now I do not hesitate to plant myself on this proposition, that the tobacco habit in its physical, mental, and moral influence is a defilement of the temple of the Holy Ghost, and therefore that the Christian church must take its stand, not by ecclesiastical laws, but by moral influence against this vice; not only the vice of using the narcotic, but also the evil of making and selling it. The Christian church must set a pure example. It must clear its own skirts or lose the respect of mankind. The Christian man who either uses, makes, or sells tobacco, is putting a temptation before the face of his own and his neighbor's boys, which is well nigh irresistible. He is especially guilty who creates and pampers unnatural demands in the community, for personal gain; just as does the proprietor of the saloon, with the difference that the tobacco store is not quite so dangerous to the peace as the saloon.

3. The reform must naturally touch first of all the Christian ministry. Not because the indulgence is inherently worse in ministers than in other Christians, but because in them the inconsistency is more glaring and makes a more public scandal, and so acts more directly against the Gospel. I rejoice to learn that the Methodist denomination are beginning to refuse license to preach to candidates who use the drug. Smoking preachers and theological seminaries have dishonored the Christian calling long enough. No man who cannot or will not practice self-denial in regard to this enslaving habit, is fit to preach the duties of self-denial on this subject to other people. A Chicago writer in the Pacific Health Journal tells of a woman who would not call the minister of her church to her death bed, because "every time during her illness that he had entered the room to bring the consolations of the blessed Gospel of love, peace, and purity, there came also with him the strong and unmistakable fumes of tobacco. To whisper into her dying ear the words of Jesus the Savior on the breath of tobacco was more than the dying saint could complacently bear." How can a minister of Christ respect either his manhood or his ministry if he advises the boys of his congregation to avoid the bitter bondage of the cigar, and then goes into his back yard or the foul

stable of the railway train and gives the lie to his advice. The old Scotch woman who objected to a minister's wearing a mustache because she "didna like to hear the word o' God come whizzin through hairs," may have been over-fastidious, but it is a dictate of clean, religious sentiment to object to hearing the "word o' God come whizzin through" lips tainted with the evidence of a filthy self-indulgence.

Aside, however, from the greater publicity of the minister's example, the demand is just as imperative that the Christian layman should abandon the habit as the Christian minister. We agree entirely with Professor Phelps that "The distinction is not a wise one which forbids it to clergymen more imperatively than to laymen." That is not a healthy type of religious faith which lays the clergy under prohibitions which are not thought necessary in regulating the conduct of other men. "Tobacco," says the Professor, "is neither for food nor drink, and so far as I know it is not medicine except to a sick sheep. An immense and increasing number of Christian believers condemn the habit as being unsympathetic with the imitation of Christ. The drift of the noblest and purest civilization is palpably adverse to a usage which so distinctly subordinates mind to matter, soul to body."

4. We must proceed on the supposition that to the Christian especially, the abandonment of the habit is possible. The shrinking from the self-denial involved in reform is a piece of cowardice unworthy a Christian soul. Fichte says, "A man can do what he ought to do, and when he says he cannot, he will not." It is idle for men in ordinary health of body and mind to say they cannot give up tobacco or that the deprivation would kill them. In many of our penitentiaries tobacco is not allowed to smokers,

and after fifteen or twenty days they are all right, appetite returns and health is better. Reformation will seldom if ever come by moderation. It comes by total abstinence. The prayer offered by an earnest New England deacon was just the prayer for tobacco users, "O Lord give us grace to know thy will and grit to do it."

Instead then of crippling our wills, instead of defiling this mysterious temple of the Spirit of God, let us stand in awe of it; let us purify and adorn it with the beauty of holiness. All spiritual agencies, all books, all churches, all social and moral reforms, are but the scaffolding to build this temple for the indwelling of God. These shall pass away, but it must stand forever. Let us rebuild, if the temple has fallen into ruin, as did the rebuilders of the ancient temple, who stood in the midst of mocking tempters, working with one hand while holding the weapon of defense in the other, and toiling "from the rising of the sun, till the stars appeared."

Chapter XV:
Christ's Appeal to the Heroism of Young People

THE SERIES of articles which closes with this number, began with this proposition: that "the secret of Christian victory is not repression, but inspiration. We kill the devil by awaking the angel in the heart." We are not to fight the good fight of faith on the low plane of the defensive, but are to go out and conquer by an aggressive campaign. Our aim in calling attention to the topics we have been discussing has not been simply to point out perils to the Christian life, but, while recognizing their reality, to indicate the source of inspiration and the motives which naturally appeal to all that is best in the hearts of young people. It is fitting, therefore, that we should close with the topic indicated above. We have talked much about Paul. Let us now turn to Christ. Our Lord pointed out both the perils and the encouragements of the Christian life in a single sentence: "In the world ye shall have tribulation; but be of good cheer, I have overcome the world." It is worthy of notice that "tribulation" does not mean simply the ordinary disappointments and sorrows of human life. The meaning of the Greek word is that of pressure or hindrance, the condition of one in a "tight place." Our English word "tribulation," comes through the Latin from the word "tribulum" a threshing machine, consisting of a wooden frame studded with sharp iron teeth. To be in tribulation is to be under the "tribulum." In both cases it means opposition, the pressure of the world spirit upon the Christian life. But we are not to speak now of the opposition, but of the Redeemer's "good cheer." From behind the shadow the still, small Voice is always sounding, full of hope and strength to the weariest of us all, "Be of good cheer, I have overcome the world!"

What Christ brought into the world was not merely a new evidence-of the world's guilt and need, but a divine hope. He saw the worst that the world contained, and yet he said, "Be of good cheer." Hope is power. Discouragement is paralysis. A false optimism and a false pessimism are both to be shunned. The one defeats Christ's divine purpose by a blind and selfish indifference to man's need of redemption; the other by an equally blind and selfish doubt as to God's remedy. It is looking too exclusively on the dark side, and overlooking Christ's ground of "good cheer" that embitters so many reforms.

The true Christian cannot be a pessimist or a cynic. The hopeless task is not laid on him of discovering a remedy for the woes of earth. His task is simple. He has only to apply the infallible remedy he has. It is not the mere analysis and exposure of the nature of sin after the manner of the moral philosopher that he is chiefly concerned with. It is rather to look on society with a Christ-inspired confidence in these three divine forces of this universe: Faith, Hope and Love, and so to be ready to suffer for society rather than to upbraid it. The gospel is not now a mere experiment. The world believes in its power. It is a cheering sign of the times that what wicked men are really, though unwittingly, crying for is Christ's Golden Rule, and that what philanthropists are aiming now to secure is simply to Christianize wealth, and laws and theories of Political

Economy. Therefore, "Be of good cheer."

Now it is quite evident that whatever purposes to insure to us victory over self and the world must be something which will appeal to the highest and weightiest forces of our nature, something worthy to awaken, inspire, employ the sum total of our moral manhood, in one sublime, heroic endeavor. This is found and found only in the religion of Christ. I ask you then, to consider Christ's appeal to the heroic element in every man. What does our Lord's call to a Christian life mean? If it were merely a call to repression, if it were only a doctrine of doubt or of "don't," if it were only to protect yourselves, it must inevitable fail. But it means infinitely more than that. As a young man standing among young men, Christ calls them to walk in his luminous steps, with all that those steps involved, with the divine suggestion to be of good cheer.

The first thing, then, is to get rid of the low, mean, dishonoring view of Christ that his religion is weak and unmanly. Jesus is the hero of the ages, and his call, when understood, touches and thrills all that is noblest in every man. Any man who says Christ's call does not inspire him either does not understand it, or he confesses that he is on a low and hopeless plane of moral manhood. The call to be a Christian is a call to self-control. Is self-control a sign of weakness? No. It is the one source of real power. "He that hath no rule over his own spirit is like a city that is broken down and without walls." Such a city lies there in a hostile country, open to the incursions of every arm that passes through the land, the camping ground of every Bedouin tribe, the lair and the prey of every wild beast. What a picture of feebleness! What a description of some young men in society to-day! On the other hand, "He that

ruleth his own spirit is greater than he that taketh a city."
The grandest sight society has to offer is that of a young
Christian standing among all the allurements of earth,
denying himself because he loves and is loyal to Christ.
Now I say, if there is any principle in man that responds
to a call which involves the hardship of self-government,
if there is a chord in the human bosom that vibrates under
the touch of a noble aim and a great purpose, Christ's call
appeals to that.

Again, is not every true man thrilled and fascinated
by a sublime example of self-sacrifice for others? That is
the second ground of Christ's appeal to the heroism of
young men. What is it that thrills and awes the soul as
we read the story of Gethsemane? Is it the divine man's
self-surrender to the divine will, and to the necessities of
a divine mission of love. It is the voluntary qualifying of
himself for an aggressive movement to save, not himself,
but mankind. And the noblest specimens of heroic life
the world knows anything about, have been the result
of that spirit caught from Christ, in the hearts of young
men. Christ's call, then, is no call to a petty profession, to
a soft-handed church membership. Weakness? Was that a
sign of weakness, when, according to Canon Farrar, in the
presence of 80,000 spectators assembled to see the gladiators fight, a Christian young man leaped into the arena and
cried, "Ye shall not fight!" He knew what the act involved.
He is hissed down. The gladiators pierce him with their
swords. His body is kicked aside. The games go on and
the people shout applause. "Yes," says the historian, "they
go on; but for the last time. By that act of heroism men's
eyes were opened; and because one poor young man had
Christian courage, one more habitual crime was wiped

from the annals of the world." Christian self-sacrifice for a great cause, combined with self-restraint, is " the highest form of self-assertion," the very essence of manliness. Are young men and women open to the touch of the sublime and heroic? Then Christ must win them.

But it is said we are riot called to such high deeds in these days. I reply, it may take as lofty a type of heroism persistently to resist the insinuations of worldliness in the church to-day and loyally to represent Christ, as it did to meet Paul's mob at Jerusalem or that young man's mob in Rome. Besides, to make a voluntary self-sacrifice, even for a matter of very subordinate importance, is always ennobling. No one appreciates that more than young men. The athlete endures hardness, refrains from dissipation, adopts frugal habits, gives up his wine and cigar, and in every way keeps his " body under," that he may overcome in a temporary physical contest, and that is ennobling. It fires his imagination. He is more of a man every way for the discipline. How much grander the appeal when a similar self-denial is demanded for the redemption of man. To respond to Christ's call is to make a double alliance, first with the Divine Person, second with a divine cause. The Divine Person calls us to his side and bids us take up the divine cause, with the great words, "Be of good cheer, I have overcome." He says: "The cause I ask you to assume is one which will keep you abreast of all progress, because it is a movement which arrays itself against all wrong. It will furnish you with endless stimulus to loftiest endeavor. It will save you while saving the world. But it will engage every fiber of your being. He that would save his life shall lose it. If you are worthy, come up to me and conquer. To struggle nobly, to conquer self, to help the needy, to bind up broken hearts, to open blind eyes, to rescue the fallen, even if you should struggle in vain, would be a mighty inspiration to all true men; but this is no vain attempt, no losing game. It is as sure as the Father's throne. I ask you to throw your consecrated manhood into this cause and to stand with me, confident of the result. "In the world ye shall have tribulation, but be of good cheer, I have over-come the world."

Who will say that is not divinely alluring to the generous, heroic spirit of young men and women? It is not the Christian but the worldling or the shirk who becomes a "milksop." We are not called to remain weaklings, like a city broken down and without walls. We are called to become a robust spiritual force, to rise up and face a grand future. Not manly to be a Christian? Paul was a Christian when he said, "None of these things move me." Stephen was a Christian when under the shower of stones he looked up and saw Jesus on the right hand of God, and cried: " Lord, lay not this sin to their charge." Martin Luther was a Christian. Chinese Gordon was a Christian. Elijah P. Lovejoy was a Christian. Howard, standing at sundown on Cemetery Hill with his empty sleeve pinned to his shoulder in front of the "Louisiana Tigers," was a Christian. John Brown was a Christian. "You are a game man, Captain Brown," said the Southern sheriff, while in the wagon going to the place of execution. "Yes," said Brown, " I was brought up so. It was one of my mother's lessons," and then walked cheerfully to the scaffold, thankful to be allowed to die for a great cause. To a friend who said to him: "If you can only be true to yourself to the very end, how glad we shall all be," he answered: "I cannot say, but I do not think that I shall deny my Lord and Master, Jesus

Christ." But why do I talk to you of these? Look at Jesus himself. See the way He overcame. Think of the contrast between him and the spirit of the times in which He lived! Look at the great world with its grand antiquity, its hoary traditions, its magnificent institutions, its captivating rituals, its systematized doctrines, its proud philosophies, its splendor of learning and littleness, its tyranny of culture and fashion, its royalty of emptiness and show; and then see the despised Nazarene, with only a dozen penniless fishermen at his back! There they are, a poor handful; but wielding the thunderbolts of God! There they are, braced against the world spirit of the ages like the cliffs of Katahdin against the oncoming sea. They are leagued with God and standing for truth and for man, and thus they overcome.

Now what I urge is this, that no young man or woman is ever called of Christ to anything less or lower than that. Wherever we stand in the scale of moral being, Christ's call touches us at our highest point and says, "Come up higher." "These things have I spoken that in me ye might have peace. In the world ye shall have tribulation, but be of good cheer, I have overcome the world." I do not think that young men will ever come to Christ in great numbers till they get this exalted view of the Christian life; but when they do get that, I believe they must and will respond.

And now, Christian readers, farewell. This great, inspiring life of Jesus Christ is the life to which you are to allure and win the men and women about you. Do not belittle it. Do not be ashamed of it. Do not exhibit merely its depressing side. Show it as it is in Jesus.

Take up His banner and bear it onward. Do not trail it in the dust. It is the symbol of victory. It may cost you something now to take it up, but the day is coming when to have spoken for Christ, to have toiled and suffered and borne witness in His cause, will be your crown of glory. The fact that can never be blotted out of your history, is that *you need Christ and that Christ needs you.* "Now the God of hope fill you with all joy and peace in believing that ye may abound in hope, through the power of the Holy Ghost." The best thing that I could wish for myself and for you, would be that we might all be able to say of ourselves in our heart of hearts what the poet has represented Paul as saying of himself:

> "Christ! I am Christ's; and let the name suffice you,
>   Aye, for me too, he greatly hath sufficed.
> So, with no winning words I would entice you,
>   Paul has no honor and no friend but Christ,
>
> "Yes, without cheer of sister or of daughter,
>   Yes, without stay of father or of son,
> Lone on the land and homeless on the water,
>   Pass I, in patience, till the work be done.
>
> "Yet not in solitude, if Christ a-near me
>   Waketh him workers for the great employ,
> Oh, not in solitude if souls that hear me
>   Catch from myjoyance the surprise of joy.
>
> "Therefore, O Lord, I will not fail or falter,
>   Nay, but I ask it, nay, but I desire;
> Lay on my lips the embers of the altar,
>   Seal with the sting and furnish with the fire.

THE BEASTS OF EPHESUS

"Quick, in a moment, infinite forever,
  Send an arousal better than I pray,
Give me a grace upon the faint endeavor.
  Souls for my hire, and Pentecost to-day.

"Flash from our eyes the glow of our thanksgiving,
  Glad and regretful, confident and calm.
Then through all life and what is after living,
  Thrill to the tireless music of a psalm.

"Yea, through life, through death, through sorrow
        and through sinning,
  He shall suffice me, for he hath sufficed;
Christ is the end for Christ was the beginning,
  Christ the beginning, for the end is Christ."